Timesaver Intermediate Listening

N COLLEGE LEARNING CENTRE

Edited by Judith Greet

Teacher's reference key

Time

A small clock on each page
tells you approximately
how long each activity should take.

Level

The number of stars on each page tells you the level of each activity

Students with two years of English

Students with two–three years of English

Students with three–four years of English

Listening tracks

There are two CDs. The top number relates to the CD;
the lower number to the track.

SCHOLASTIC

MARY GLASGOW

Contents

★ Students with 2 years of English

★★ Students with 2-3 years of English

★★★ Students with 3-4 years of English

Teacher's Notes

Introduction

Intermediate Listening contains 42 communicative worksheets based around authentic and semi-authentic listenings graded from low to high intermediate level. Each self-contained lesson includes pre-listening, while listening and post-listening tasks to ensure full exploitation and understanding of each recording. Worksheets can be selected by topic, function and listening skill, and act as a useful supplement to any intermediate coursebook. Answers are included in the Teacher's Notes.

★ Students with 2 years of English

1 Making Films (page 16)

Listening aims: Listening for gist – reordering pictures
Listening for specific information – find words in a wordsquare

New vocabulary: scriptwriter, producer, actor, actress, director, lighting, photography, editor

Pre-listening

1 Write students' ideas on the board.

Listening

2 Students look at the pictures. Get them to describe each picture. Write any new words on the board. Pupils listen and order the pictures.
Answers: 1 e) 2 d) 3 d) 4 a) 5 b)

Ask pupils again who the most important person is. Have any of them changed their minds – why?

3 Pupils listen again and find eight words connected to film making in the wordsearch.
Answers: scriptwriter, producer, actor, director, lighting, photography, actress, editor

Post-listening

4 Explain that we say *make a film* and *make a decision* but *do me a favour*. Tell students that they have to learn these expressions – there are no fixed rules. Advise them to create their own lists and add to them when they meet new expressions. This table will start them off.
Answers: *do* – homework, the washing up, your best, your hair, good, exam; *make* – fun of someone, an effort, progress, a noise, an appointment, a change

5 In small groups, pupils discuss their all-time favourite film. Each group can only suggest one title – they will have to persuade each other of the merits of their film. Elicit titles from each group and see if the class can agree on an all-time favourite film.

2 How Are You Feeling? (page 17)

Listening aims: Listening for gist – match pictures and conversations; **Pronunciation** – -*ed* endings

New vocabulary: worried, excited, frightened, annoyed, bored, relaxed, exhausted, depressed, confused, interested

Pre-listening

1 Pupils discuss the questions in pairs. Elicit answers.

Listening

2 Play this twice if necessary. Ask some comprehension questions, e.g. *What is wrong with Rebecca? Why?* etc.
Answers: 1 d) 2 b) 3 c) 4 e) 5 a)

3 Read the three words in the table and explain why they are in each column (because of the 'ed' sound). Students listen and complete the columns. Check answers.

Answers: /t/ - relaxed; /d/ - worried, frightened, annoyed, bored; /ɪd/ - excited, exhausted

Post-listening

4 Students draw a picture to describe someone who is relaxed or worried.

5 Give students three to five minutes to think of other words. They can compare their answers with a partner before you check with the class.
Possible answers: /t/: stressed, shocked /d/: terrified, scared, tired, satisfied, surprised, embarrassed, amazed /ɪd/: disappointed

6 Allow 3-5 minutes. Monitor as students are working. Elicit feelings from the students.

3 Love (pages 18 & 19)

Listening aims: Listening for specific information– choose between words; **Listening for gist** – matching pictures and conversations; multiple matching.

New vocabulary: head over heels in love, break someone's heart, treat, brace, embrace, pest, sentimental

Pre-listening

1 You could also get students to match the expressions to the pictures before checking answers.
Answers: red roses, break somebody's heart, fall in love, love at first sight, head over heels in love, first love, love letter
Break somebody's heart would make them sad.

Listening

2 Give students time to read through the poems before you play them. They could choose the words at this point and then check them when they listen. Teach any new vocabulary.
Answers: a) red, sweet b) face, night c) coffee, tea
d) heart, mine e) pie, car f) fine, do my best

Post-listening

3 Elicit their favourite poem. Ask if they can tell you any others in English. Discuss what they think of Valentine's Day.

Listening

4 Play the recording once.
Answers: 1 d) 2 a) 3 b) 4 c)

5 This is a multiple matching activity. Students need to read the questions first and then listen again.
Answers: b) 3 c) 2 d) 1 e) 3 f) 2 g) 4 h) 1 i) 3 j) 2 k) 1 l) 4

6 Explain that they heard people making suggestions in the conversations. See if students can tell you any phrases. If necessary students listen again.
Answers: a) What about this one? Yes. It's all right.   b) How about this one with the rabbit on it? Yes, that's sweet.   c) Why don't you take her out to a posh restaurant? That's a good idea.

7 Read through the situations with the students. They should try to use the structures in Ex 6.

4 Losing Weight (pages 20 & 21)

Listening aims: Listening for specific information – filling in a form; understanding advice

New vocabulary: put on weight, lose weight, calorie controlled diet, burn calories, snacks

Pre-listening

1 Discuss the pictures with the class, asking them to describe what they can see.

Listening

2 Students read through the questionnaire before listening and completing it.
Answers: a) Brown b) 9th March c) 3-4 hours d) very rarely
e) very rarely f) Playing computer games g) crisps h) chicken
i) fruit

3 Give students time to discuss what advice they would give Alison. Write up the suggestions on the board.
Students then listen to the interviewer giving Alison advice. Is it the same as theirs? Do they think the interviewer's advice is good?

Post-listening

4 Students ask and answer the questionnaire. They then give each other feedback by offering advice. If you wish, you can make this into a written activity where students can write a letter of advice to their partners. This can be done for homework.

5 Video Games (page 22)

Listening aims: Listening for specific information – choosing correct sentences; reordering sentences

New vocabulary: influence, message, ache, bend, hand-eye coordination

Pre-listening

1 Put students in small groups and let them discuss the question for 3-4 minutes. Take a vote and write the numbers on the board.

Listening

2 Students read through the sentences before listening.
Answers: a) P b) P c) P d) x e) P f) x g) P h) x

3 Students try to reorder the sentences and then listen again to check.
Answer: c) e) b) a) f) d)

Post-listening

4 Students should discuss each statement and either agree or disagree with it. They do not have to agree with each other but should explain their points of view. After five minutes, ask students which one they agree/disagree with most strongly.

5 Elicit why students have changed their minds.

6 At the Airport (page 23)

Listening aims: Listening for specific information – following instructions; **Listening for gist** – saying where something is

New vocabulary: check-in desk, duty-free shop, bar, passport control, newsagent's, hand luggage, shoulder strap, diary

Pre-listening

1 Discuss answers with the students.

Listening

2

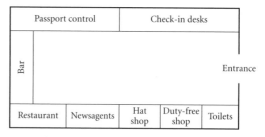

Passport control		Check-in desks	
Bar			Entrance
Restaurant	Newsagents	Hat shop	Duty-free shop	Toilets

3 Students listen once.
Answer: It must be in the hat shop.

Post-listening

4 Check vocabulary.
Answer: c)

7 Helping a Friend with a Problem
(page 24)

Listening aims: Listening for specific information – reordering information

New vocabulary: eating disorder, anorexia, low self-esteem, concentrate, emotional problems, uptight, share, feel blue, get you down, frown, solution

Pre-listening

1 Either discuss as a class or let students work in pairs to discuss before sharing ideas as a class.

Listening

2 You might like to discuss eating disorders with the students first and ask them what they know. Students read through the symptoms before listening.
Answers: 2, 1, 3, 5, 4

3 Students may need to listen twice.
Answer: *See recording script*

Post-listening

4 Are there songs they listen to when they are upset or happy?

8 New York City (page 25)

Listening aims: Listening for gist – matching people and photos; **Listening for specific information** – true or false

New vocabulary: bookings, go on a tour, history, spend time, island

Pre-listening

1 Elicit answers. Write some of their ideas on the board, especially new vocabulary.

Listening

2 Discuss the photos with the students first.
Answers: a) Mum b) George c) Dad d) Anna

3 Students read the sentences through first.
Answers: a) T b) F c) F d) T e) F f) F g) T h) F

Post-listening

4 You could let students discuss whether they think it is right or not to visit the site of the Twin Towers.

9 Text and Phone Messages (pages 26 & 27)

Listening aims: Listening for gist – matching questions and answers; **Listening for specific information** – completing a table; choosing the correct words

New vocabulary: get in touch, notes, high-tech version, strict rules, ring tone, signal, make contact

Pre-listening
1 Elicit other text messages from the students.
Answers: 1 c) 2 e) 3 f) 4 h) 5 g) 6 a) 7 d) 8 b)

Listening
2 1 b) 2 a) 3 e) 4 d) 5 c)

3 Students listen and complete the table.
Answers: a) Saturday b) 0208-478961 c) 7:00 d) 01299-309255 e) Anna f) 0786-876890 g) Ellie h) 08789-678998

Post-listening
4 After writing their excuses, studen sit back to back and leave the message. The message taker tells the class the message. The class chooses the most imaginative excuse.

Listening
5 If you wish, let students read the song through first and try to predict the words.
Answers: home, loud, standing, go, clear, hear, feeling, with, can, got, seemed, seconds, Rome

10 Schools in Britain (pages 28 & 29)

Listening aims: Listening for specific information – completing a table, completing a passage;
Pronunciation – syllables

New vocabulary: secondary school, scholarship, keyboards, flute, informal, uniform, detention, strict, boarding school, competitive, inspiring, experiments, swot, nursery school

Pre-listening
1 Elicit ideas and encourage discussion.

Listening
2 The students will hear four different people talking about their schools. They take notes to fill in the table.
Answers: Sophie *type of school:* large secondary state school *doesn't like* homework & music practice every night, relaxed, informal; *enjoys:* no uniform; **Jack** *type of school:* private boys' school; *doesn't like:* school uniform, too strict, chemistry; *enjoys:* playing football at breaktime; **Ryan** *type of school:* boarding school; *doesn't like:* misses family, stupid rules, being treated like children; *enjoys:* living with friends; **Louise** *type of school:* drama school; *doesn't like:* nothing; *enjoys:* everything, drama & music lessons and the more usual subjects

3 Explain the concept of syllables by giving some examples first, e.g. teacher (2), school (1), exciting (3). Look at the example on the page. Students write the number of syllables.
Answers: a) 2 – stress is on the 1st syllable b) 2 – 1st syllable c) 3 – 1st syllable d) 1 e) 2 – 1st syllable f) 3 – 2nd syllable g) 3 – 1st syllable h) 4 – 2nd syllable i) 3 – 2nd syllable j) 2 – 1st syllable

4 Ask students to read through the passage before they listen and try to predict what might fill the gaps. Check any new vocabulary. Play the recording.
Answers: b) 7 c) 5 d) 5 e) 16 f) 18 g) ten h) science i) geography j) music k) 8 l) university m) 20

Post-listening
5 Elicit ideas from students.

6 Discuss any new vocabulary.
Answers: religious studies drama biology maths chemistry information technology geography English art physical education

11 Being a Detective (page 30)

Listening aims: Listening for gist – choosing pictures

New vocabulary: victim, weapon, shot, truncheon, handcuffs, whistle, iron bar, shoplifting, robbery, burglary, terrorism, blackmail, hijacking, rape, mugging, fraud

Pre-listening
1 Give students 1-2 minutes to complete this.
Answers: handcuffs, truncheon, whistle, notebook.
Items police don't carry: iron bar, knife

Listening
2 **Answers:** 1 a) 2 a) 3 b) 4 a) 5 a)

Post-listening
3 Play the recording again if necessary.
Answers: man, He, was, before, gun, heard

4 **Answers:** shoplifting, robbery, burglary, murder, terrorism, blackmail, hijacking, rape, mugging, fraud
The sentence is: *It must have been his brother-in-law.*
If you wish, discuss the crimes further with the students, asking them to explain them.

5 They could do this in pairs in the classroom or individually for homework.

12 Food (page 31)

Listening aims: Listening for specific information – completing a table; **Listening for gist** – reordering pictures; responding to questions

New vocabulary: curry, apple crumble, custard, sophisticated, portion, lamb chop, mashed potato, veggie

Pre-listening
1 Students work in pairs and discuss what they ate the previous day.

Listening
2 Check the words in the box before students listen. Check answers.
Answers: Sophie *breakfast:* cornflakes; *lunch:* chicken burger; *dinner:* burger, chips and peas. **Ryan** *breakfast:* toast with butter *lunch:* chicken curry, apple crumble; *dinner:* pizza. **Jack** *breakfast:* Weetabix; *lunch:* chicken and chips; *dinner:* lamb chops; chocolate cake. **Louise** *breakfast:* croissants; *lunch:* tuna sandwich, smoked salmon; *dinner:* vegetable lasagne, chocolate cake

3 Ensure students know what is on the trays.
Answers: 1 d) 2 c) 3 a) 4 b)

Post-listening
4 In this section, students have to speak to the recording. Play it a couple of times and choose different students to answer. Then let them practise in pairs, one of them being the assistant. They can change the dialogue slightly if they wish. Choose a few pairs to act out their dialogue to the class.

13 Black Rights in America (page 32)

Listening aims: Listening for specific information – adjectives and numbers

New vocabulary: graceful, popular, dignified, heroic, charming, chatty, witty, inspiring, boastful, detest, mindless, legend, sacrifice, slave trade, slavery, protest, abolish, discrimination, cemetery

Pre-listening

1 Students can work in pairs. Encourage the use of English-English dictionaries. Elicit ideas.

Listening

2 Elicit what students know about Muhammad Ali before they listen. Play it twice.

Answers: 1 2 4 6 7 9 11 12

3 Elicit from students what they know about the history of black Americans and teach any relevant vocabulary. Tell the students to write numerals not words.

Answers: a) 1500   b) 300   c) millions   d) 1775-1783
e) 1955   f) 382   g) 1960

Post-listening

4 Students should discuss in groups before having a class discussion.

14 Summer Camp (page 33)

Listening aims: Listening for gist – ordering pictures; matching titles; **Listening for enjoyment**

New vocabulary: pack, influence, irritable, licence, crash, ankle, first aid kit

Pre-listening

1 Students discuss their plans for the holidays. Are they pleased with their plans or not?

Listening

2 Let the students listen to the play for enjoyment first. Ask them to tell you what they thought of it. Play it again for students to do the exercise.

Answers: 1 e)   2 c)   3 a)   4 d)   5 b)   6 f)

3 Read what happens to Andy. Discuss these with the class at this point before playing the recording.

Answers: 1 c)   2 b)   3 a)

Post-listening

4 Go through the expressions with the students. Give them a different situation to practise if you wish, e.g. tell them you can't decide whether to go to the US or the UK for a holiday and ask them for advice.
In pairs, students decide what advice to give to Andy and Gemma. Elicit ideas from different pairs.

5 Give students 10-15 minutes to write the dialogue. Choose groups to read it aloud.

★★ Students with 2-3 years of English

15 Anna's Story (pages 34 & 35)

Listening aims: Listening for specific information – true/false; multiple choice; answering questions

New vocabulary: cuddle, share, unsterilised, pierce, blood transfusion, by accident, lottery, paradise, crucial, precaution, irreversible, telepathy, hostile, desperate, frightened, angry, hopeful, worried, selfish, moody, two-faced, apologetic, unfriendly, bigoted, prejudiced

Pre-listening

1 This exercise is to find out how much the students know about AIDS. Let them work through it in pairs.

Answers: a) P b) x c) x d) x e) P f) P g) x h) x i) P

Listening

2 Students read through the statements first.

Answers: 1 T 2 T 3 F 4 T

3 Students read through the options.

Answers: 1 c) 2 b) 3 c) 4 a) 5c)

4 Students read through the questions.

Answers: a) No, she thought of it but didn't actually do it.
b) Like rubbish.   c) Yes, but she denied it at first.
d) Her mother who them told everyone's else's mother.
e) She went to a group.   f) It brought them closer.

Post-listening

5 Students read through the adjectives and match them with the characters.

Answers: Anna – desperate, frightened, angry; **Anna's mother** – hopeful, worried; **Karen** – selfish, moody, two-faced, apologetic; **Karen's mother** – unfriendly, bigoted, prejudiced

16 Getting a Job as an Au Pair (pages 36 & 37)

Listening aims: Listening for specific information – answering questions

New vocabulary: au pair, agency, make an appointment, babysit, the tube, collect

Pre-listening

1 Discuss what the class knows about being an au pair. Let them try to complete the section of the letter.

Answers: I work twenty-five hours a week and babysit two nights a week. I have to look after the children, clean the house do the washing and ironing and sometimes do some cooking. I don't pay for my room or my food and the family pays me fifty pounds a week. I also go to English classes.

Listening

2 Students read through the questions first and make sure they understand them before listening.

Answers: a) Wednesday   b) 7pm   c) 5 and 6
d) a quarter past nine   e) 3pm   f) 6pm   g) 2 nights
h) Yes, but it is small (although it has its own bathroom)
i) 98 Devonshire Road   j) Turnham Green

Post-listening

3 Talk about how important it is for students to give as much information as is sensible if they are asked a question in an intevieuw or exam situation.

Suggested answer: Tania because she is more communicative.

Answers: a) ✔   c) ✔   d) ✔   e) ✔

4 Students then work in pairs and practise the questions. This should take about 2 minutes each – not 10 seconds!

5 Students work in groups of three and roleplay the interview between Mr and Mrs Palin and Tania. Monitor as they are working. Choose some groups to perform in front of the class.

17 New Zealand (pages 38 & 39)

Listening aims: Listening for specific information – choosing correct options; **Listening for gist** – matching

New vocabulary: fantastic, scary, fab, amazing, disgusting, awesome, beautiful, walking boots, mud, agriculture, clubbing, paragliding, bungee jumping, brain, sulphur

Pre-listening

1 Discuss the photos before doing the exercise.

Answer: 4 and 8

Listening

2 Give students time to read through the options first and go over any new vocabulary.

Answers: 1 a) 2 a) 3 b) 4 a) 5 a) 6 b) 7 b) 8 a) 9 b)

3 Play the recording again if necessary.

Answers: New Zealand – beautiful; **Number of sheep** – amazing; **Helicopter ride over Fox's Glacier** – awesome; **Some of the activities to do** – scary; **Bungee jumping** – fantastic; **Swimming with the dolphins** – fab; **The smell at Rotorua** – disgusting

Post-listening

4 Revise how we would write it in speech, i.e. in a different tense and with speech marks. Students write the conversation.

Answers: "Have you got any walking boots in your bag?"
"Yes."
"Have they got mud on them?"
"Yes."
"Can I clean them for you?"

5 Adam said that they had hired a car and driven to Fox's glacier. He told me that everyone went to bed early in New Zealand. He said that Queenstown was amazing. He told me he had gone black water rafting. He said he had been swimming with dolphins. He said that he could really recommend New Zealand. He told me you could see lots of whales around the coast of New Zealand. He told me Rotura had been very smelly. He said he didn't think Nicola would go back to New Zealand. He told me he wanted to go back next year.

6 Let pupils discuss their view of New Zealand. If they don't want to go there, where would they like to go?

18 Love Isn't Easy (page 40)

Listening aims: Listening for gist – matching sentences and letters; **Listening for specific information** – listening for phrasal verbs

New vocabulary: sympathetic, jealous, introvert, extrovert, flirtatious, selfish, egotistical, sensitive, accuse, go-karting, lie, split up

Pre-listening

1 Ask the students to discuss the question, using an English-English dictionary if necessary. They should then report back and give reasons for their answers, thereby explaining the words.

Listening

2 Answers: a) 3 b) 1 c) 4 d) 2 e) 3 f) 4 g) 1 h) 2

3 Answers: 1 split up 2 get on (well) 3 go out with
4 think about 5 ask out

Post-listening

4 This can be done for homework.

19 Stress (page 41)

Listening aims: Listening for specific information –
completing sentences; word building

New vocabulary: relaxed, laid-back, assignments, proud,
pressure, grades, ambitious, impressive, hippies, pushy parents,
yoga, stress, sympathetic, embarrassed; imagine

Pre-listening

1 Students discuss this in small groups then as a class.

Listening

2 Students read through the sentences before listening and
choosing the correct answers.

Answers: 1 b) 2 a) 3 b) 4 a) 5 c) 6 b) 7 c) 8 a) 9 c)

3 This exercise will help students develop their word building
skills. When they learn a new word they should be aware of
the other words connected to it.

Answer: ambitious, relaxed, proud, stress, sympathetic,
embarrassed; imagine, agree, train, feel, expect, study

Post-listening

4 In this exercise students have to discuss a number of items
and reduce them by agreeing on the best ideas. They each
start with ten adjectives – five to describe an ideal school and
an ideal teacher. They reduce them to six in total. They give
their suggestions and the rest of the class agrees or not. Try
to get the whole class's list down to five for each part.

20 Internet Nerds (page 42)

Listening aims: Listening for specific information – ticking
true statements; **Pronunciation** – phonemics

New vocabulary: secret, copy, set up a business,
sophisticated, catchy, venture capitalist, borrow, lend

Pre-listening

1 Students can do this in pairs.

Listening

2 Ask students to read the statements through before they
listen. Check any new vocabulary.

Answers: True statements: 1 2 4 5 8 9

3 Students listen and write the words they hear. They then
match them with the phonemic script.

Answers: married relaxed business andwiches
1 b) 2 c) 3 a) 4 d)

Post-listening

4 Choose two students to read the dialogue. Ask them to give
other examples with *borrow* and *lend*. Students do the
exercise.

Answers: a) borrow b) lend c) borrow d) lent e) lend
f) borrow

5 Give students 10-15 minutes to do this.

21 Australia (page 43)

Listening aims: Listening for gist – matching information with
names; **Listening for specific information** – multiple choice

New vocabulary: immigrants, coral, incredible, scuba dive,
inhabitant, miniature, current, lizard, toad, weird, hot air
balloon, mosquito

Pre-listening

1 Elicit what students know about Australia and discuss the
photos with the class. Find out if anyone has been there.

Listening

2 Check they understand *immigrants, the Outback, convicts.*

Answers: 1 Great Barrier Reef 2 Surfing 3 Aborigines
4 Sydney 5 Outback 6 Convicts 7 Ayers Rock 8 immigrants

3 Students read the questions before they listen to the next
part of the recording. Ask them to try to guess which the
answers could be. When they have listened, they should try
to justify their answers. You will probably need to play the
recording twice to enable them to do this.

Answers: 1 b) 2 c) 3 b) 4 c) 5 a)

Post-listening

4 The tourist must ask as many questions as possible and the
other needs to give as much advice as possible.

22 Holiday Romance (page 44)

Listening aims: Listening for gist – reordering pictures;
Listening for specific information – dictation

New vocabulary: puppy love, cupboard love, adore, blind,
cottage, sunbathe, romantic, excursion, heart-broken

Pre-listening

1 Ask students if they know of similar expressions in their own
language.

Answers: 1 b) 2 a) 3 b) 4 a) 5 b) 6 a)

Listening

2 Encourage the class to predict what the story will be about.

Answers: a) 6 b) 3 c) 2 d) 5 e) 1 f) 4

3 Tell the students they are going to do a dictation but with a
difference. They have to read the text on the page and then
listen and try to remember what they heard. They must not
write while they are listening. Give them a few minutes to
write what they can remember before listening again.

Post-listening

4 Students write the story for homework.

23 What would you do? (page 45)

Listening aims: Listening for specific information –
matching adjectives, matching statements

New vocabulary: confident, wimp, courageous, black pudding,
blood, disgusting

Pre-listening

1 Check with students they know what the different food is.
Ask them what they would be happy to eat. Discuss which
food they won't / can't eat.

Listening

2 **Answers:** fashionable, cool, disgusting

3 Read through the list with the students. Ask for other ways
of saying some of these expressions, e.g. *a) I'd call the
police. b) I ran after the boy. c) That wasn't very clever.
f) I'd say I was a vegetarian. g) I'd say I felt ill.*

Answers: a) Tom and Asif b) Mel c) Tom d) Asif e) Asif
f) Asif g) Asif and Mel h) Tom

Post-listening

4 Read through the situations with the students first. Give
them five to seven minutes to discuss what they would do
in each situation using *I'd...* Ask pairs to report back and
vote on the best ideas.

24 Addictions (pages 46 & 47)

Listening aims: Listening for specific information – multiple choice; **Pronunciation** – syllables

New vocabulary: alcoholism, drug addiction, sexist, criticise, alcohol, alcopops, off-licence, legalise, prescribe, homeless

Pre-listening

1 Let students work in pairs and write down all the things people can be addicted to, e.g. smoking, alcohol, drugs, chocolate, TV, coffee, shopping etc.

Listening

2 Ask students to read through the questions before listening to the recording. Check any new vocabulary. Play it twice.

Answers: 1 b) 2 b) 3 c) 4 b) 5 a)

3 Students read the words and decide how many syllables there are. Do not correct their answers yet. Play the recording and let them check their answers.

Answers: drinking (2) criticised (3) advertisement (4) later (2) wanted (2) difficult (3) closed (1) addicted (3) opinion (3) understanding (4)

Post-listening

4 Point out that if a verb follows a preposition, it has to be the –ing form.

Answers: a) of b) at c) to d) of e) for f) for g) from h) of

5 Elicit suitable answers, agreeing or disagreeing with the statement. Read through the examples with the students. Let students discuss the statement in small groups. Ask one student to report back.

6 Allow students about 10 minutes to discuss the statements and then have a class discussion.

25 Parents (pages 48 & 49)

Listening aims: Listening for specific information – ticking information and sentences heard

New vocabulary: glum, give someone a hard time, hassling

Pre-listening

1 Students report back to the class after discussion.

Listening

2 Students read through the sentences before listening. You could ask them to say what things they don't like about living with their parents.

Answers: 1 4 6 7 10

3 Students read through the sentences first.

Answers: 1a 2b 3b 4a 5b

Post-listening

4 Let the students work in pairs to create the sentences.

Answers: b) She's always using my mobile. I wish she wouldn't.
c) She's always telling mum on me. I wish she wouldn't.
d) She's always giving me advice. I wish she wouldn't.
e) She's always copying my homework. I wish she wouldn't.
f) She's always playing her awful music loudly. I wish she wouldn't.

5 Elicit the answers to the questions – No, he didn't.; No, he isn't.; No, he isn't.

Answers: b) Lucy wishes she had bought the CD in Freeman's.
c) Chris wishes he hadn't eaten the whole chocolate cake.
d) Liz wishes she hadn't gone skating. e) Ed wishes he hadn't gone to town by bus. f) Oliver wishes he hadn't taken the dog for a walk.

6 Elicit advice from the students.

Suggested answers
Lucy: If I were you, I'd take the CD back to Brown's and ask for your money back. **Ed:** Why don't you report it to the police? **Oliver:** You should talk to your girlfriend.

26 Teenage crime (pages 50 & 51)

Listening aims: Listen for specific information – completing a text with words, choose the correct sentences

New vocabulary: boot camp, shoplifting, mugging, arson, vandalism, rape, murder, ex-offenders

Pre-listening

1 Read through the situations with the students, making sure they understand them. Allow the students to work through the situations in pairs or in small groups to decide the punishments.

Listening

2 Students could give suggestions of what the solution could be. They then listen and see if they were right.

Answer: boot camps

3 Discuss the photo before students do the exercise.

Answers: 1 across 2 two 3 murder 4 crime 5 guns
6 experiencing 7 reality 8 shock

4 Students listen and choose the correct sentences.

Answers: 1 a) 2 b) 3 a) 4 b)

Post-listening

5 Students read and decide if the statements are true or false.

Answers: a) T (Parents do it to show children what could happen to them if they break the law.) b) F (They have to wear uniforms.) c) F (There is silence.) d) T e) F f) T g) T h) F

6 Answers: a) has committed b) has spent c) has been hiding d) has been sleeping; has been stealing e) has not told f) has questioned g) has met h) have been teaching

7 Students discuss whether boot camps are a good idea or not.

27 Advertising (pages 52 & 53)

Listening aims: Listening for specific information – finding adjectives; choosing the correct option

New vocabulary: fascinating, star, assignments, depressed, adore, irresistible, wicked, chat, ming vase, emperor, exquisite

Pre-listening

1 Elicit all answers, writing new or difficult words on the board, before students listen.

Listening

2 Do this advert by advert. Read through the questions for advert 1. Play the recording, students choose the answers. Check the answers. Repeat for Adverts 2 and 3.

Answers: Advert 1 – 1 a) 2 b) 3 a) 4 a); Advert 2 – 1 a) 2 b) 3 b) 4 a) 5 b); Advert 3 – 1 b) 2 a) 3 b)

Post-listening

3 Give some examples with –ing and –ed adjectives, e.g. *I went to see a film last night – it was amazing. I was amazed by the special effects.* Read through the example sentence. Check they understand the adjectives for the other sentences. Students complete the sentences.

Answers: b) exciting, fascinating c) interesting d) worried e) confusing f) boring, tired, relaxed

4 Students discuss their favourite advert at the moment. Elicit ideas from the class. Have a vote on the best advert.

5 Give students 10-15 minutes to prepare their advert before showing them to the rest of the class.

28 The Lost Boy (pages 54 & 55)

Listening aims: Listening for gist – matching adjectives with characters; **Listening for specific information** – answering true or false

New vocabulary: mistreated, alcoholic, flame, garage, vomit, chores, quarter, pool table, retreat in a shell, surge, blurt, slash marks, bruise, grab, mumble, swivel, garbage, drain, creak, disbelief, caring, liar

Pre-listening

1 a) Students look at the picture and work in pairs to suggest what the story might be about. Elicit suggestions. Write any new vocabulary on the board.
b) Students look at the words in the box and decide if they want to change their stories. Elicit suggestions.

Listening

2 Read through the words with the class and make sure they understand them. Explain that Dave is the young boy in the picture. Mark is someone who works in a bar which Dave goes into. Students listen to the whole story and match the words with the characters.

Answers: Dave – hungry, upset, scared, ashamed;
Dave's mother – cruel, drunk, liar, unloving; **Mark** – caring, concerned, kind, thoughtful

3 Students read through the questions and answer the ones that they can. Play the recording again for them to check their answers and complete the exercise.

Answers: a) T b) F c) F d) T e) F f) T g) F h) F i) T j) F k) T l) F m) F

Post-listening

4 Students work in groups of five to act out the play.

5 Elicit suggestions. Vote on the best ending.

6 Elicit ideas to explain the words and phrases:
Answers: a) fizzy drink b) dustbin c) I'm not surprised.
Answers: a) queued; sweets b) loo c) holiday d) destroyed

★★★ Students with 3-4 years of English

29 The Environment (page 56)

Listening aims: Listening for specific information – responding to statements

New vocabulary: litter, regard, uncool, uninhabitable, squirrel, asthma, allergy, convenient

Pre-listening
1a Give students time to discuss.
Answer: They can all be recycled.

1b Students can work in groups to come up with as many ideas as possible, e.g. empty jars can be used as vases, to keep buttons etc in, to store food, to use when making jam, etc. etc.

Listening
2 Read through the sentences before students listen to the recording. Play it through twice.
Answers: a) This might be true for some teenagers, but the main reason teenagers don't pick up litter is because it isn't cool anymore.   b) If everyone thought like that no one would do the simple things we can all do to protect the environment. c) But if there was a law that you had to recycle, more recycling bins would be available and it would be more convenient. d) This might be true but I don't think statements like this make people take action. It's best to say there's a danger the world will become uninhabitable then people realise that it's going to affect them.   e) You might not believe there will be any significant changes in our lifetime, but you wouldn't want your children to suffer because you've been selfish.

Post-listening
3 This can act as revision of the perfect tenses.
Answers: b) have been talking   c) has been polluting d) have been recycling   e) has thought   f) have been slowly destroying; have not thought   g) have been suffering; has got h) have never taken

4 Encourage students to discuss the advantages and disadvantages of the ideas mentioned as well as thinking up their own ideas. Each group could be asked to think of the best three ideas to tell the rest of the class.

30 Growing up in the USA (page 57)

Listening aims: Listening for specific information – answering comprehension questions; completing questions

New vocabulary: conservative, progressive, recess, outgoing, inhabitants

Pre-listening
1 Let students discuss the question and write down as many advantages and disadvantages they can think of. Elicit ideas from the whole class and discuss.

Listening
2 Explain that they are going to hear an American talking about where she grew up. Students read through the questions before listening.
Answers: 1 b), c), f), h), j)   2 Her mother was working.   3 a) shopping, b) making dinner for her grandfather.   4 a) playing with her brother and sister, b) going to the beach with her family   5 a) They ate lunch together, b) They played together at recess.   6 a)   7 c)   8 b)   9 Someone who is an extrovert and makes friends easily.   10 a)

3 Play the recording again. Stop after each question and get the students to complete the questions. They then work in

pairs to ask and answer the questions (boys obviously need to change question 'c' if speaking to another boy). Elicit answers from the class.
Answers: a) Where did you grow up? Can you tell me a little bit about it?   b) What's your earliest memory of when you were very young?   c) Were you the sort of person who had lots of friends or were you a 'best friend' girl?   d) Were you shy as a child? How would you describe yourself?

Post-listening
4 Students discuss the advantages and disadvantages of being an only child. Elicit ideas from the class and continue the discussion.

31 Humour (pages 58, 59 & 72)

Listening aims: Listening for specific information – answering questions; playing a game

New vocabulary: alien, checked, cell, getaway, giggle, sense of humour, ironic, slapstick, goofy, inopportune

Pre-listening
1 Give students 3 or 4 minutes to complete the exercise.
Answers: 1d)   2e)   3a)   4f)   5b)   6c)

Listening
2 There are a variety of questions – make sure students read through them before they listen. Play it twice.
Answers: 1a) laugh at jokes and things in the world b) laugh at yourself   2b)   3 get along with her friends 4 English: e, j; American: d, g   5b)   6b)   7 a) silly b) goofy 8 trips over something

Post-listening
3 Give students five minutes to discuss before having a class discussion. Encourage them to tell the class a funny scene from a film or a joke.

Listening
4 Answer: saucepan

Post-listening
5 Make a set of cards with mystery words on. These can be words that students have learnt in recent lessons. Here are some possible words: umbrella, helicopter, referee, spectacles, dictionary, flowers, bicycle, elephant, clock, postman, biscuits, mango, etc. There is also a set on page 72 to photocopy and cut out. Play the game as a class first then in smaller groups. Once one of the topics has been used, it cannot be used again. They can score through it on their sheet.

32 Americans Abroad (pages 60 & 61)

Listening aims: Listening for specific information – answering questions

New vocabulary: impressions, stick out like a sore thumb, accommodate, assimilate, customs, overseas

Pre-listening
1 Give students 3-4 minutes to discuss before eliciting ideas from the whole class.

Listening
2 There are a variety of questions again here. Students need to read through them before listening. Play the recording twice.
Answers: 1c)   2 She thought that it was the right way.   3 get

with the times   4 d)   5 c)   6a)   7c)   8a)   9c)   10a) egotistical
b) self-centred   11d)   12 fall   13c)   14 a) race b) culture
c) place d) language   15 b)   16 caught up in   17 b) d) g)

33 Childhood (page 62)

Listening aims: Listening for gist – ordering pictures;
Listening for specific information – multiple choice

New vocabulary: perilous, witch, persecuted, gravel,
irrational, seed, poppies, illicitly, in bloom, cart, ambitious,
bolted, accelerate

Pre-listening

1 Give students 3-5 minutes to discuss then choose a few to
tell their stories.

Listening

2 Teach some vocabulary before students listen, especially
cart, poppy.
Answers: c e a d f b

3 Students read the questions before listening.
Answer: 1b)   2 c)   3 b)   4a)   5c)   6a)   7a)   8a)

Post-listening

4 Discuss what kind of language they would use in a letter
of complaint – formal. Discuss how the letter would start
and end (Dear Mr and Mrs James; Yours sincerely). Also
discuss how to start the letter (I am writing to complain
about …) and any linking words that could be used (First,
Then, Moreover, etc). This exercise could be done in class
or for homework.

34 American Culture (page 63)

Listening aims: Listening for specific information – finding
false statements

New vocabulary: culture, picturesque, novelty, sky-scrapers,
buzz, vibrant

Pre-listening

1 Give students three minutes to do the exercise. After they
have compared their lists, elicit some suggestions from them.

Listening

2 Students should read the sentences through first.
Answers: Stephen 2; Becky 3; Georgina 3

Post-listening

3 Answers: 1d)   2i)   3l)   4a)   5g)   6k)   7c)   8j)   9b)   10f)
11h)   12e)
4 This exercise will encourage students to use a variety of
vocabulary rather than just 'cool' or 'nice'.
Answers: films – exciting, dramatic, brilliant, gripping;
clothing – fashionable, stylish, trendy, designer;
food – delicious, scrumptious, mouth-watering, tasty

35 Poetry (pages 64 & 65)

Listening aims: Listening for specific information – multiple
choice; **Listening for enjoyment** – a poem

New vocabulary: ignore, defend, distinction, wage war,
foreign policy, mercenary, frail, slight, shattered, crouched, cave

Pre-listening

1 Elicit views about poetry from the class.

Listening

2 Students read through the questions before listening.
Answers: 1b   2b   3c   4b   5b   because she doesn't believe in

killing people for political reasons   6a   7c   8a to point out
the difference between two things   b to help those people
who want to fight   c to go to war   d to fight   9d

Post-listening

3 Read through the words with the students, making sure
they understand them. Give them time to match the words
before using them in the sentences.
Answers: escape, recover, differ from; belong, hope, object
to; consist, accuse, approve of; concentrate, depend, insist on;
apologise, pay, search for; believe, specialise, succeed in
a) belong to   b) searched for   c) concentrate on
d) accused of   e) believe in   f) escaped from

Listening

4 Students could practise reading the poem after they have
completed it.
Answers: see transcript

5 Allow students to discuss in groups before discussing as a class.

36 Body Piercing (pages 66 & 67)

Listening aims: Listening for specific information –
comprehension questions; completing sentences

New vocabulary: piercings, tattoos, sorrowful, over-
impressed, reseal, discrete, ID, turn up, go off, suit, trendy,
eyebrow, frowned upon, snobbery, rebellious, pathetic,
connotations, prejudiced, threshold

Pre-listening

1 Students report back when they have had time to discuss.
You could extend the discussion to include other laws that
are affected by age, e.g. age you can drive / drink alcohol /
get married / have a job / leave school etc.

Listening

2 Ask students to read through the questions before listening.
Play the recording twice.
Answers: a) Five earrings and a nose piercing which has now
healed up.   b) Because she didn't mind when Becky had her
ears pierced without her permission.   c) She would be
prejudiced against them.   d) One of his teachers.
e) British people think women with tattoos are unladylike.
f) It doesn't suit her.   g) Body piercings have connotations of
rebelliousness. Older people might think people with body
piercings are punks.

3 Play the recording of the questions through completely then
play again with pauses so that students have time to write.
Answers: a) What do you think when you see someone who
is completely covered in tattoos? What's your initial reaction to
that?   b) Do you feel any differently if it's a woman who's
covered in tattoos, as opposed to a man?

4 Answer: You shouldn't decide on a person's character by
the way that they look.
Students can work in pairs to discuss the questions in exercise 3
before discussing as a class.

Post-listening

5 Students can use dictionaries if you wish.
Answers: sorrowful, illegal, rebellious, over-impressed,
disgusted, unladylike, painful
Students work individually to complete the sentences.
b) unladylike   c) painful   d) illegal   e) impress   f) disgusted
g) rebellion

6 Students could listen again but they should be able to do
this without listening.
Answers: a) about   b) from   c) from   d) on   e) in   f) on

37 Clubbing (page 68)

Listening aims: Listening for specific information – advantages and disadvantages; ticking a list. **Predicting**

New vocabulary: in the mood, socialise, gig, energetic, packed, a breath of fresh air, bouncers, blame someone for, look forward to

Pre-listening

1 Students can practise present simple with adverbs of frequency with this exercise. Elicit sentences such as *Most people in the class usually meet friends on Saturday evening. They often go to the cinema.* etc.

Listening

2 Discuss with the class what they think advantages and disadvantages of going clubbing would be (either from experience or from what they have heard from others). Write the points on the board. Ask students to listen and say whether their points were mentioned. They then listen again and write down any further points.

Answers: Advantages – You can 'let yourself go' and enjoy yourself; clubs are good if you are feeling energetic and want to do some dancing. **Disadvantages** – It's difficult to talk to people; clubs get very crowded; you can't go out to get any fresh air; there are long queues; bouncers can refuse to let you in.

3 As they have heard the recording twice already, students may be able to do this exercise now. If they find it hard, play the recording again.

Answer: a) b) d) f)

Post-listening

4 When students have had time to complete the sentences, ask for ideas.

38 Hooliganism in Britain (page 69)

Listening aims: Listening for specific information – completing sentences; **Predicting**

New vocabulary: lad culture, birds, violence, hooliganism, secular, institution, spur, unite

Pre-listening

1 Give students an example, e.g. football player, before they complete the puzzle. Discuss what the connection is between football and hooliganism.

Answers: stadium, boots, team, pitch, kit, shirt, hooligan, player, shorts, match

Listening

2 Read through the sentences with the class. Ask students for ideas of how the sentences might finish. Play the recording twice.

Answers: a) Stephen thinks that there is a lad culture in Britain <u>but that it isn't bad</u>.   b) He thinks that it is just <u>a fashion</u>.   c) Georgina thinks that the lad culture has been created by <u>magazines</u>.   d) She doesn't think it is representative <u>of young guys in Britain</u>.   e) Becky thinks that perhaps young people get obsessed with football because they don't <u>have anything to believe in</u>.   f) Georgina doesn't think football should be a bad thing. The World Cup and the Euro Cup <u>bring people together</u>.

Post-listening

3 Encourage students to defend their choices.

4 Give students time to discuss the statements in groups and then report back their ideas to the whole class. Write their ideas on the board and vote for the best three.

39 Careers (page 70)

Listening aims: Listening for specific information – gap fill

New vocabulary: performance, caberet, precarious, self-employed, money is tight, option, mod cons, scrimping and saving, pursue, mortifying, destitute,

Pre-listening

1 This is an open exercise where students can suggest careers but must be able to justify their choices.

Listening

2 Give students time to read through the paragraphs, checking vocabulary before they listen twice.

Answers: a) voice b) stories c) self-employed d) steady e) childhood f) actor g) book h) statistics i) pursue j) education k) responsibility l) remember

Post-listening

3 Give students 5-7 minutes to ask and answer as many questions as possible. Elicit examples.

4 Elicit some examples, other students can make different suggestions. Ask the students if they think they would be happy with the careers chosen for them.

40 The Internet (page 71)

Listening aims: Listening for gist – matching; **Listening for specific information** – comprehension questions

New vocabulary: resource, acclimatise, inept, log on, pathetic, IT-illiterate, enriched, diversity, regulate, verification, chatroom, escapism

Pre-listening

1 After the students have discussed the questions in pairs, have a class discussion to establish the views on the Internet.

Listening

2 Elicit reasons from students explaining why they are like one of the speakers. Would they like to change?

3 Students read the questions before they listen again.

Answers: a) Because his family's last phone bill was very expensive.   b) It isn't very important to her. She doesn't use it very much and she needs Stephen's help to log on.
c) You can't tell if the information you find is truthful.
d) Occasionally there are awful occurrences, for example people have met up with someone they chatted to and they've been violent. But if you're careful, Internet chatrooms are nothing to worry about.   e) Her age and her looks.
f) Because it's escapism and it's fun.

Post-listening

4 Use this synopsis to talk with the students about the dangers of chatrooms. Use any instances you have heard of to tell the students about. If there isn't time to write the story in class, give it for homework. Ask the students to write between 120 and 180 words.

1 Making Films

1 Work in pairs and discuss: Who is the most important person in a film? Why?

2  Listen to some teenagers describing how you make a film and put the pictures below in order.

a)

b)

c)

d)

e)

3 Listen again and find eight words connected to making films in the word search.

```
S T S T A B G E R J K A
P R G N I T H G I L O A
C V X A S R W E R H L C
H I D S O O A P O P E T
S C R I P T W R I T E R
T H E A T C O O S T M E
R C V S B A N D M K I S
O R T Y U C V U B N O S
T P O E R O T C E R I D
I I O S C R U E P L T A
D P H O T O G R A P H Y
E D G X P L Z W R T G H
```

a) .... e) ....

b) .... f) ....

c) .... g) ....

d) .... h) ....

4 In the listening you heard these sentences:

Making a movie is very expensive.

Some directors make all the decisions themselves.

In some expressions we use *make* and in others we use *do*. For example:

The actor did a dance and sang a song in the audition.

homework   fun of someone
the washing up   your best
an effort   progress   your hair
good   a noise   an appointment
exams   a change

Write the words in the box in the correct column – *do* or *make*.

DO	MAKE
homework	

5 Work in groups. Write down your all-time favourite film. Which is the most popular film in your group? Which is the most popular film in your class?

2 How are you Feeling?

1 Work in pairs. What are you interested in? What makes you depressed?

2 Listen and match the pictures to the five conversations. Write the number of the conversation next to the corresponding picture.

3 How do you pronounce these adjectives? Write them in the correct column, then listen to check.

worried   excited   frightened   annoyed   bored   relaxed   exhausted

/ t /	/ d /	/ ɪd /
depressed	confused	interested

4 Two of the adjectives are not used in the conversations. Draw a picture of one of them and show it to your partner. Can they guess your adjective?

5 Add five more words to the table. Compare your answers with others.

6 Work in pairs. Describe what is happening in these photos. Talk about how you might feel in these situations.

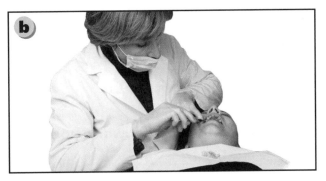

3 Love

1 Match the words in the two columns to make phrases connected to love.

red	letter
break somebody's	in love
fall	heels in love
love at	love
head over	heart
first	roses
love	first sight

Which one would make you sad?

2 🎧 **1/4** **Listen to the love poems and choose the correct words to fill the gap.**

1) Roses are .... *(red / dead)*
Violets are blue
Sugar is .... *(a treat / sweet)*
And so are you, Stu!

2) It was love at first sight
When I saw your .... *(brace / face)*
I can't sleep at .... *(night / fight)*
Without your embrace.

3) I love .... *(coffee / lemonade)*
I love .... *(tea / peas)*
I love Robby
Next to me.

4) My love, I don't mind
That you've stolen my ....
(heart / part)
You'll always be .... *(mine / fine)*
Because I love you, Bart.

5) I love you more than the sun in the sky
I love you more than apple ....
(tart / pie)
I love you more than a brand-new
.... *(car / cap)*
I love you more than a chocolate bar ...
err... maybe not
But I love you lots!
Marry me, Daniel Potts

6) Peter, be my valentine
And every day I'll feel so ....
(fine / kind)
Don't say no, please say yes
And I will always ....
(be a pest / do my best)

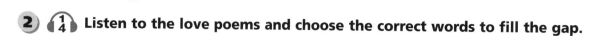

3 **Discuss with a partner which poem you would choose to write on a Valentine's card.**

4 Listen to the Valentine's Day conversations and match each conversation to a picture.

a

b

c

d

5 Listen again and match the conversations with the actions.

In which conversation do the people ...

a) buy a card with an animal on it .... *1* ....
b) decide to buy someone a meal ....
c) offer to help ....
d) spend less than £5.00 ....
e) make a booking ....
f) go to a florist's ....
g) ask someone to do something ....
h) buy two cards the same ....
i) not smoke ....
j) buy a present for their girlfriend ....
k) buy some stamps ....
l) sound surprised ....

6 Listen to these suggestions and replies from the conversations. Complete them.

a) .... this one? **Yes. It's** ....

b) .... this one with the rabbit on it? **Yes,** ....

c) .... her out to a posh restaurant? **That's a** ....

7 Work in pairs.

Situation 1: Student A can't decide what to do on Valentine's Day. Student B, make some suggestions. Student A: choose one of the suggestions.

Situation 2: Student B can't decide what to buy their girlfriend/boyfriend for Valentine's Day. Student A, make some suggestions. Student B: choose one of the suggestions.

4 Losing Weight

1 **Match the sentences and the pictures.**

1 She put on weight when she was studying for her exams.
2 She lost weight when she gave up fatty foods.
3 She is on a calorie controlled diet.
4 She's trying to burn calories by going to the gym every day.

c

a

b

d

2 **Alison was interviewed about her habits. Listen and fill in the gaps in the form or tick the correct option.**

Name   Alison (a) ....
Age   15
Date of birth   (b) 1985

(c) **How much sport do you do each week?**
0 hours ☐   1-2 hours ☐   3-4 hours ☐   More than 4 hours ☐

(d) **How often do you cycle or walk instead of going by car?**
Never ☐   Very rarely ☐   Sometimes ☐   Often ☐   Always ☐

(e) **How often do you do jobs around the house?**
Very rarely ☐   Sometimes ☐   Often ☐   Always ☐

What are your hobbies?
Watching TV
(f) ....

What do you usually eat for breakfast?
Biscuits or (g) ....

What do you usually eat for lunch?
Chips

What do you usually eat for dinner?
Fish or (h) .... with potatoes and vegetables or pasta.
(i) .... or yoghurt.

Do you eat snacks between meals?
Sometimes. Crisps, chocolate or biscuits.

3 Work in pairs. What advice would you give Alison to help her lose weight?

a) ....

b) ....

c) ....

d) ....

e) ....

Now listen to the interviewer. Is his advice similar to yours?

4 Work in pairs. Ask and answer the questions in the questionnaire.
What advice would you give your partner?

Name ....

Age ....

Date of birth ....

How much sport do you do each week?
O hours ☐   1-2 hours ☐   3-4 hours ☐   More than 4 hours ☐

How often do you cycle or walk instead of going by car?
Never ☐   Very rarely ☐   Sometimes ☐   Often ☐   Always ☐

How often do you do jobs around the house?
Very rarely ☐   Sometimes ☐   Often ☐   Always ☐

What are your hobbies?
....
....
....

What do you usually eat for breakfast?
....

What do you usually eat for lunch?
....

What do you usually eat for dinner?
....
....

Do you eat snacks between meals?
....

HARROW COLLEGE
HH Learning Centre
Lowlands Road, Harrow
Middx HA1 3AQ
020 8909 6520

5 Video Games

1 Do you think video games are good or bad? Take a class vote and write the results in the boxes.

Number of people who think
video games are good ☐

Number of people who think
video games are bad ☐

2 🎧 Listen to some teenagers talking about video games. Tick (✓) the things that you hear them mention about video games and put a cross (✗) next to the things that you don't hear them mention.

a) They're fun. ☐

b) They help you make friends. ☐

c) They improve your memory. ☐

d) They help you do your homework. ☐

e) Some people play them all the time. ☐

f) They make you want to steal cars. ☐

g) They're boring. ☐

h) They are addictive. ☐

3 🎧 Listen again and put the sentences in the order you hear them.

a) They show you how to steal or shoot a gun. ☐

b) Do you like video games? ☐

c) Everybody always talks about video games. ☐

d) But video games have some advantages. ☐

e) I love football and basketball video games. ☐

f) It gets boring. ☐

4 What do you think? Work in pairs and discuss these statements.

> Video games are fun.

> Video games send a bad message to kids.

> You don't learn anything from video games.

> Video games don't influence me.

> Video games help improve your memory.

> Video games are educational.

5 Take a class vote again. Has anyone changed their minds? Are video games good or bad?

Number of people who think video games are good ☐

Number of people who think video games are bad ☐

6 At the Airport

1 You have two minutes to write down who or what can you see at an airport, **e.g.** *pilot*

2 🎧 **1 10** Listen to someone describing the airport and write the names of the different places on the plan.

Entrance

3 🎧 **1 11** Rebecca is at the airport. She is very worried because she has lost her bag and her plane is going to leave soon. Rebecca's friends decide where it must be.

	YES	NO
In the toilets?		
In the duty-free shop?		
In the hat shop?		
In the newsagent's?		
At the check-in desk?		
In the bar?		

4 Which is Rebecca's handbag? Read the description and match it to a bag.

It's a black leather handbag with a shoulder strap. It has got my ticket in it but not my passport. There is a purse with two credit cards and quite a bit of money. My house key is in my bag along with my diary with lots of important information. There's a comb, a mirror and some lipstick. Oh, and a photo of my boyfriend.

a

b

c

d

7 Helping a Friend with a Problem

1 What kinds of problems do teenagers have? What do you do when you have a problem?

2 🎧 ¹/₁₂ Listen to this interview with an eating disorders expert. Put these symptoms in the order you hear them.

- ☐ losing a lot of weight very quickly
- 1 always thinking about food and the calories in it
- ☐ trouble sleeping
- ☐ feeling depressed
- ☐ feeling cold

3 🎧 ¹/₁₃ This song is telling you what to do if you have a problem. Each verse has four lines but they are not in the correct order. Listen to the song and put the lines in the correct order.

A PROBLEM SHARED

If you're having problems ☐   Your homework gets you down ☐
Are you feeling all right? ☐   Your parents make you frown ☐
Hey there. You look sad ☐   You hate your sister and ☐
You mustn't be uptight ☐   You love your friend's brother ☐

If they're shared between two ☐   *(Chorus)*
Famous people do too ☐   Find a solution and ☐
But problems seem smaller ☐   Ask your friends for advice ☐
Everyone has problems ☐   Your life will feel so nice ☐

Chorus   Don't worry, be happy ☐
A problem shared
is a problem halved   Don't stay at home and cry ☐
If you share your problems   Get a friend to listen ☐
They get smaller each day   It's easy if you try ☐
If you share your problems   Talk your problems over ☐
They will soon go away
                                   (Chorus)
Write to a problem page ☐
That'll stop you feeling blue ☐
They tell you what to do ☐
Problems with your parents? ☐

4 Discuss. Do you think this song would be helpful if you had problems? Why?/Why not?

8 New York City

1 You have two minutes to think of as many things connected to New York City as you can.

2 🎧 **1 14** Listen to this family planning a trip to New York. They are talking about what they want to do there. Look at the pictures. Match the speakers (Mum, Dad, Anna and George) with the pictures of what they want to do.

a ....

b ....

c ....

d ....

3 **True or false?**

a) Mum suggests booking things on the Internet. ☐

b) Anna finds history boring. ☐

c) George is enthusiastic about going on a tour. ☐

d) Father thinks there's a lot to see in New York. ☐

e) Father will love shopping in New York. ☐

f) Anna says that you can see for four miles from the top of the Empire State Building. ☐

g) Father suggests going on a boat. ☐

h) All of New York City is on an island. ☐

4 Work in pairs. Discuss where you would like to go in New York City. Make some suggestions and plan a day. Don't forget to stop and have something to eat!

Use these expressions from the recording:

Do you know where you want to go?

I really like ...ing

Maybe we could ...

How about ...

I don't mind .... but ....

9 Text and Phone Messages

1 What do these text messages mean? Match the text messages with their meanings.

1 U R L8

2 L8R

3 TXT

4 2

5 2NITE

6 XLNT

7 B4

8 GR8

a) excellent ☐
b) great ☐
c) you are late ☐
d) before ☐
e) later ☐
f) text ☐
g) tonight ☐
h) to ☐

2 🎧 1/15 You will hear the answers to the five questions below. Listen and match the names with the questions.

1 Ellie ☐
2 Simon ☐
3 Kate ☐
4 Ms Anderson ☐
5 Mr Harrison ☐

a) How do your parents feel about mobile phones?
b) How much money do you spend on your phone per week?
c) Do you think text messaging is bad for spelling?
d) Does your school have rules about mobile phones?
e) What do your parents say about text messaging?

Now work in pairs. Ask and answer the questions for you.

3 🎧 1/16 Another way of contacting someone is by leaving a phone message. Listen to these messages and complete the grid.

NAME	MESSAGE	PHONE NUMBER
1 Simon	Do you want to go to the football match on **(a)** ....?	**(b)** ....
2 Dad	Ring before **(c)**	**(d)** ....
3 (e)	Call as soon as possible.	**(f)** ....
4 (g)	She's going to be late.	**(h)** ....

4 Imagine you have been invited to a party that you don't really want to go to. Phone up and leave a message, giving a good excuse why you can't come. Your partner will listen and write a message.

> *My pet rabbit is very ill and I can't leave it by itself.*

> *I kicked a football through a window and I have to repair it.*

> I have a piano exam on Monday and my piano teacher says I must get as much sleep as I can.

5 **Listen to the song and circle the words you hear.**

MOBILE WORLD

Talking on the phone in this mobile world
No-one's ever **home / alone** in this mobile world
Everyone's got something to say, make yourself be heard
Say it **loud / slow** and say it clear, every single word

Chorus
Talk, talk, talk, talk
Here in this crowded room
Talk, talk, talk, talk
Trying to get a message through
Talk, talk, talk, talk
Ring tone plays a tune
Talk, talk, talk, talk
The whole world is calling

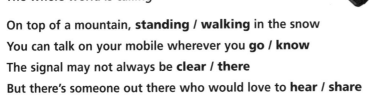

On top of a mountain, **standing / walking** in the snow
You can talk on your mobile wherever you **go / know**
The signal may not always be **clear / there**
But there's someone out there who would love to **hear / share**

(Chorus)

Making contact when you like and never **feeling / being** alone
Distance is no problem **with / for** a mobile phone
You can text a message, you **can / could** use your voice
When you've got a mobile phone, you've **got / made** a choice.

(Chorus)

All around the world, which **seemed / was** so far away
You can get through in **seconds / no time**, night and day
Talking on the phone, in this mobile world
From Australia to **Rome / Bonn**, in this mobile world

6 **Work in pairs. Do you think there are any disadvantages to having a mobile phone?**

10 Schools in Britain

1 Do you think British schools are different to your school? Work in pairs and write down any differences you think there might be. Think about areas such as age, clothes, subjects and exams.

2 (1/18) Listen to four British teenagers talking about their schools. Fill in as much information as you can in the table below.

	type of school	doesn't like	enjoys
Sophie			
Jack			
Ryan			
Louise			

3 (1/19) Look at the words below. How many syllables are there in each word?

Example: music – 2 syllables
musical – 3 syllables

Now listen and write the number of syllables you hear in each word.

1	lesson	......2......	**5**	private	....	**9**	behaviour	....
2	homework	....	**6**	detention	....	**10**	study	....
3	uniform	....	**7**	chemistry	....		
4	strict	....	**8**	experiment	....		

Now listen again. This time, underline the stressed syllable.

4 (1/20) Some teenagers are now going to give you some information about the education system in Britain. Listen and complete the missing information.

State education is free but some parents pay for **a)** _private_ education.

Private school are very expensive and about **b)** .... % of British kids go to them.

Children go to nursery school from three years old to **c)** .... years old.

They go to primary school when they are **d)** .... years old.

They start secondary school at 11. Children in the UK must go to school until they are **e)** .... years old.

They can stay at school for two more years until they are **f)** .... years old.

Children at secondary school in Britain have to study **g)** .... subjects.

The main subjects are English, mathematics and **h)** .... Children must spend more time studying these subjects.

The other subjects are history, **i)** .... , art, one foreign language (French is the most usual), design and technology, physical education and **j)** ....

When they are 16 years old, students have to take General Certificate of Secondary Education exams (GCSEs) in as many subjects as they can manage, often about **k)** .... or ten.

At 18, they take A levels which qualify them for entry to **l)** .... Students in the UK specialise early, choosing just three or four subjects to study at A level.

About **m)** .... % of young people go to university or college.

5 Were you right about the differences between British schools and yours? Have you found any other differences?

6 Look at the objects below. Name them and find the relevant school subject in the wordsearch.

```
R  E  L  I  G  I  O  U  S  L  H
E  D  A  D  R  A  M  A  T  H  S
L  U  C  R  E  R  R  F  U  C  I
U  C  I  C  I  T  E  A  D  E  L
B  A  S  Y  G  O  L  O  I  B  G
V  T  Y  S  I  L  G  N  E  W  N
S  I  H  M  A  T  H  S  S  T  E
N  O  P  R  T  S  I  M  E  H  C
I  N  F  O  R  M  A  T  I  O  N
G  T  E  C  H  N  O  L  O  G  Y
O  Y  H  P  A  R  G  O  E  G  U
```

....

....

....

....

....

....

....

....

....

....

....

....

What is your favourite subject?

11 Being a Detective

1 **Find six items in the word snake – which two do not belong to a policeman?**

handcuffsironbartruncheonwhistleknifenotebook

2 **Look at the pairs of pictures. Tick (✓) the picture in each pair that you hear the detective talking about.**

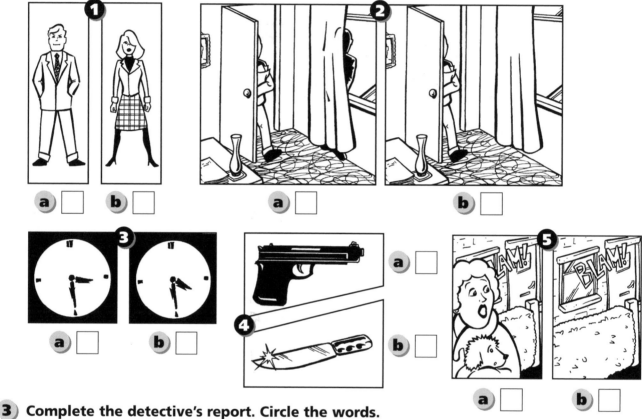

3 **Complete the detective's report. Circle the words.**

The killer was a *man / woman*. *He / She was / was not* in the house when the victim arrived.

The crime happened *before / after* 4.00. The killer used a *gun / knife*.

The neighbours *heard / did not hear* the shots.

4 **Find ten crimes in the wordsquare.**

When you have found the words, you will be able to see a sentence which will tell you who the murderer must have been according to the detective.

S	H	O	P	L	I	F	T	I	N	G	I
T	M	M	U	S	Y	R	E	B	B	O	R
T	B	U	R	G	L	A	R	Y	H	A	A
V	E	G	B	E	E	U	N	H	I	S	P
B	R	G	M	U	R	D	E	R	O	T	E
M	S	I	R	O	R	R	E	T	H	E	R
I	N	N	B	L	A	C	K	M	A	I	L
L	A	G	N	I	K	C	A	J	I	H	W

5 **Write a story explaining why the murder happened.**

12 Food

1 Discuss with a partner what you ate yesterday. Tell your partner if you think they ate healthily or not!

2 🎧 1/22 Listen to some teenagers talking about what they ate yesterday and complete the information in the chart. The words in the box will help you.

> lamb chops   chocolate cake   chicken curry   cornflakes   chicken burger   apple crumble
> chicken and chips   croissants   chips   smoked salmon   vegetable lasagne

	breakfast	lunch	dinner
Sophie			burger, ... and peas
Ryan	white toast with butter		pizza
Jack	Weetabix		
Louise		tuna sandwich	chocolate cake

3 🎧 1/23 Listen to Sally's family ordering their food. Put the trays in the order that you hear them: 1, 2, 3, 4.

4 🎧 1/24 Listen again to the fast food restaurant assistant's part of the dialogue. Answer her questions. You will hear a <beep> when it is your turn to speak.

Assistant:	Hello. Can I help you?
You:	*(Order a cheese burger)*
Assistant:	Would you like any fries with that?
You:	*(Order a large fries)*
Assistant:	Would you like a drink?
You:	*(Order an orange juice)*
Assistant:	Would you like anything else?
You:	*(Order a doughnut)*
Assistant:	That's £3.75, please.

13 Black Rights in America

1 Explain the words in the box. Use a dictionary to help you.

> **a)** graceful   **b)** popular   **c)** strong   **d)** dignified
>
> **e)** interesting   **f)** heroic   **g)** charming   **h)** chatty
>
> **i)** witty   **j)** intelligent   **k)** inspiring   **l)** boastful

2 (1/25) **Muhammad Ali was a famous American boxer. He experienced racism during his career and felt very strongly about the rights of black people in America. Listen to some teenagers talking about Muhammad Ali. Circle the nine words in the above box that you hear.**

3 (1/26) **Listen to this brief history of African Americans and fill in the missing dates and numbers in the text.**

Most American blacks originally come from an area in western Africa. This area had efficient governments and a lot of its wealth came from trading. The slave trade began in the early **a)** .... For the next

b) .... years **c)** .... of black Africans were taken by ship to the USA and Latin America. During the Revolutionary War in America (from **d)** .... to ....) many Americans turned against slavery. They felt it was against human rights. However, in the south of the USA there were large farms which grew cotton, tobacco and other crops. They needed lots of workers and most of their workers were slaves. Most of the people who were against slavery lived in the north of America. This would eventually lead to a civil war between the north and the south.

After the Civil war the US government helped freed slaves to find jobs, houses and education. But as they tried to enter society, many black people found that the racism of white people made life difficult. Gradually the civil rights movement started up. In **e)** .... Rosa Parks, a civil rights activist was arrested for disobeying a city law that required blacks to give up their seats on the bus when white people wished to sit in them. Black people protested by refusing to ride on the buses. They protested for **f)** .... days. The protest ended when the city abolished the bus law.

The most famous civil rights leader was Martin Luther King. He asked African Americans to protest peacefully. During the early **g)** .... the efforts of the civil rights groups ended discrimination in many public places including restaurants, hotel and cemeteries.

4 **Discuss. Muhammad Ali was a famous sportsperson who stood up for black rights. If you were famous, would you support a particular cause? What would it be and why? Can you think of advantages or disadvantages of famous people being involved with a cause?**

14 Summer Camp

1 What are you planning to do in the summer holidays? Tell your partner.

2 Listen to this play called Summer Camp. Put the pictures in the correct order.

a

b

c

d

e

f

3 Listen to the three suggestions for an ending to the play. Match the ending to what happens to Andy.

Ending 1   **a)** Andy tells a lie. ....

Ending 2   **b)** Andy feels happy and confident. ....

Ending 3   **c)** Andy is arrested. ....

4 Discuss with a partner what advice you would give Andy and Gemma.

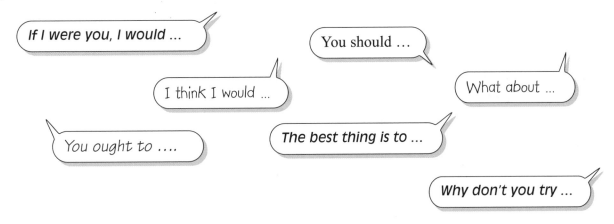

If I were you, I would ...

You should ...

I think I would ...

What about ...

You ought to ....

The best thing is to ...

Why don't you try ...

5 Work in groups of three. Imagine you are either Andy or Gemma. Your parents have found out what happened. Create a dialogue.

15 Anna's Story

1 **What do you know about HIV and AIDS. Tick the statements which are correct.**

You can get AIDS:

a) if you share a toothbrush with someone who has AIDS. ☐

b) if you share a plate of food with someone who has AIDS. ☐

c) if you cuddle someone who has AIDS. ☐

d) if you go swimming with someone who has AIDS. ☐

e) if you use an unsterilised needle. ☐

f) if you have your ears pierced using unclean tools. ☐

g) if you shake hands with someone who has AIDS. ☐

h) if you take care of someone who has AIDS. ☐

i) if you have an infected blood transfusion. ☐

PART ONE

2 🔊 **Listen to Anna telling the first part of her story and mark the sentences below with F if they are false and T if they are true.**

a) Many people thought the girl's mother should have told her she was HIV positive immediately. ☐

b) The girl suspected her mother was HIV positive after she listened to her telephone conversation. ☐

c) The girl's mother knew she was listening. ☐

d) The girl's mother must have told the girl's aunt she was HIV positive before she told her children. ☐

PART TWO

3 🔊 **Choose the correct answer a, b or c.**

1 When the girl's mother told her and her brother she was HIV positive ☐

a) they were not sure about the difference between being HIV positive and having AIDS.

b) the girl and her brother were hysterical.

c) the girl and her brother just sat there.

2 After a few months, the family had ☐

   a) changed dramatically.
   b) learnt a lot more about the virus.
   c) became closer.

3 The girl told Karen about her mother because ☐

   a) Karen's mother was a doctor.
   b) Karen was always kind.
   c) she was worried and needed to talk to someone.

4 When the girl told Karen that her mother was HIV positive, ☐

   a) Karen was sympathetic.
   b) Karen said she did not want to touch anything that the girl had touched.
   c) Karen hugged her.

5 The girl shouldn't have told Karen because ☐

   a) the girl's mother had told her not to tell anyone.
   b) Karen's younger brother had heard the conversation.
   c) Karen couldn't keep a secret.

PART THREE

4 🔘 **Listen to the final part of the story and answer the following questions.**

   a) Did Anna say anything when she heard what the other girls said?

   ....

   b) How did Karen's mother treat her?

   ....

   c) Did Karen admit what she had done?

   ....

   d) Who had Karen told?

   ....

   e) How did Anna eventually manage to talk about her fears?

   ....

   f) What effect had the virus had on Anna's relationship with her mother?

   ....

5 **Match the adjectives in the box with the people in the story.**

desperate	moody	prejudiced	angry	unfriendly	two-faced
frightened	apologetic	worried	bigoted	selfish	hopeful

Anna – ....

Anna's mother – ....

Karen – ....

Karen's mother – ....

16 Getting a Job as an Au Pair

1 Do you know what an au pair does? Read this section of a letter written by an au pair. All the vowels (a, e, i, o, u) are missing. Fill them in and find out what she does.

> I w_rk tw_nty-f_v_ h_ _ rs _ w_ _ k _ nd
> b_bys_t tw_ n_ghts _ w_ _k. I h_ve t_ l_ _k
> _ft_r th_ ch_ldr_n, cl_ _n th_ h_ _s, d_ th_
> w_sh_ng _nd _r_n_ng _nd s_m_t_m_s d_ s_m_
> c_ _k_ng. I d_n't p_y f_r my r_ _m _r _ny
> f_ _d _nd th_ f_m_ly p_ys m_ f_fty p_ _nds
> _ w_ _k. I _ls_ g_ t_ _ngl_sh cl_ss_s.

Ask a partner if they would like to be an au pair. Why?/Why not?

2 🎧 (1/32) Listen to the conversation between Tania, an au pair, and Mr Palin, someone looking for an au pair. Answer the following questions.

a) What day of the week is Tania going to see the Palin family?

....

b) What time is Tania going to see the Palin family?

....

c) What ages are the Palins' children?

....

d) What time do the kids need to be at school?

....

e) What time do the kids need to be collected from school?

....

f) Until what time does Tania need to look after the kids?

....

g) How many nights does Tania have to babysit?

....

h) Would Tania have her own room? Will it be big?

....

i) What is the Palin's address?

....

j) What is the nearest station to the Palins?

....

3 **Mr Palin interviewed two au pairs, Molly and Tania.**
Read these questions and answers.
Who do you think got the job? Why?

Mr Palin:	Have you looked after children a lot?
Molly:	Yes, I have.
Mr Palin:	Can you come to see us on Thursday?
Molly:	No, I can't.

Mr Palin:	Have you looked after children a lot?
Tania:	Quite a lot. I'm the oldest of five. And I taught small children drama when I was at school. I did it as part of my work experience because I want to be a primary school teacher.
Mr Palin:	Can you come to see us on Thursday?
Tania:	Well, I usually go to evening classes on a Thursday but I suppose I could miss it this week.

Which of these sentences would you say to Molly? Tick them.
Then write two more sentences with *need to* or *don't need to*.

a) You need to get your hair cut.   ☐

b) You don't need to change your clothes.   ☐

c) You need to answer questions more fully.   ☐

d) You don't need to ask any questions.   ☐

e) You need to speak so people can hear you.   ☐

f) ....

g) ....

4 **Now ask and answer these questions with a partner.**
Answer them as fully as possible.

a) Do you like sport?

b) What book are you reading at the moment?

c) Which country would you like to visit?

d) Do you like classical music?

e) Which famous person would you like to meet?

f) Do you want to be a teacher?

5 **Roleplay the interview between Mr and Mrs Palin and Tania.**

Mr and Mrs Palin – Think about what Tania will have to do each day. What questions will you ask her?

Tania – Think of any questions you want to ask the family. Are you clear about your duties? Don't leave until you know exactly what you will have to do each day.

17 New Zealand

1 What do you know about New Zealand? Read these facts and find the two which are false.

a) The population of New Zealand is less than four million.

b) There are more sheep than people.

c) Maoris are the original New Zealanders.

d) You can't ski in New Zealand.

e) Part of *Lord of the Rings* was filmed in New Zealand.

f) The people of New Zealand are known as 'kiwis'.

g) You can see 35 kinds of whales around New Zealand.

h) Rugby is not popular in New Zealand.

2 🎧 ¹⁄₃₃ Listen to the letters from a tourist to New Zealand, Adam, and choose the correct options below.

Letter 1

1 a) The customs officer washed Adam's boots at the airport.
b) Adam washed his own boots at the airport.

2 a) The boots needed to be cleaned to protect agriculture.
b) Adam wanted his boots to be cleaned so that customs didn't stop him.

Letter 2

3 a) Adam couldn't believe how cheap things were in New Zealand.
b) Adam couldn't believe how many sheep there were in New Zealand.

4 a) Adam took a helicopter up to the top of the Fox's Glacier.
b) Adam misses London nightlife.

Letter 3

5 a) Adam has already done white water rafting and paragliding.
b) Adam has been getting up late because the nightlife is so good in Queenstown.

6 a) Adam has done a bungee jump.
b) Adam is going to do a bungee jump.

Letter 4

7 a) Adam has entered a competition.
b) Adam is whale watching in Kaikoura.

8 a) Adam went swimming with the dolphins.
b) Adam wanted to go swimming with dolphins but they couldn't find any.

Letter 5

9 a) Adam has got sunburnt in Rotorua.
b) Adam thinks Rotorua smells bad.

3 🎧 **1 33** **Listen again. Match the things Adam wrote about with the adjectives.**

New Zealand	*fantastic*
Number of sheep	*scary*
Helicopter ride over Fox's Glacier	*fab*
Some of the activities to do	*amazing*
Bungee jumping	*disgusting*
Swimming with the dolphins	*awesome*
The smell at Rotorua	*beautiful*

4 **What did the customs officer actually say to Adam? Write the conversation.**

The Kiwi customs officer asked if I had walking boots in my bag. I said yes. Then he asked me if they had mud on them. I said yes. He immediately looked at them and asked if he could clean them for me.

Customs officer: .....Do you have...

Adam: ....

Customs officer: ....

Adam: ....

Customs officer: ....

5 **When Adam gets back he tells you all about his holiday. Later that week, you meet a friend and tell him what Adam said. Read Adam's words in the speech bubbles and write down what you said to your friend. Use the verbs *say*, *tell*, etc.**

a *We hired a car and drove to Fox's glacier.*

b *Everybody goes to bed early in New Zealand.*

c *Queenstown is amazing.*

d *He went black water rafting.*

e *I have been swimming with dolphins.*

f *I can really recommend New Zealand.*

g *You can see lots of whales around the coast of New Zealand.*

h *Rotorua was very smelly!*

i *I don't think Nicola will go back to New Zealand.*

j *I'm hopefully going back next year.*

6 **Work in pairs. Would you like to go to New Zealand? Why?/Why not? Discuss.**

18 Love isn't Easy

1 **Which of these adjectives describe the boyfriend / girlfriend you would like to have?**

> good-looking   funny   sympathetic   jealous   introvert   fashionable   extrovert
>
> sensible   flirtatious   shy   understanding   selfish   egotistical   sensitive

2 **Listen to the problem page letters then match the sentences to the correct letter.**

a) I get jealous when I see her laughing with other boys.   ☐

b) She's making me choose between my friends and her.   ☐

c) She's a geek but I like her.   ☐

d) My friend will never forgive me but he's worth it.   ☐

e) I want to tell her to stop.   ☐

f) I hope I didn't hurt her feelings, shy people can be sensitive.   ☐

g) She's so insecure.   ☐

h) I know that we'd be happy together but it's a terrible thing to do to a friend.   ☐

3 **Listen again and make a word web with five phrasal verbs connected to relationships. There are clues in the box.**

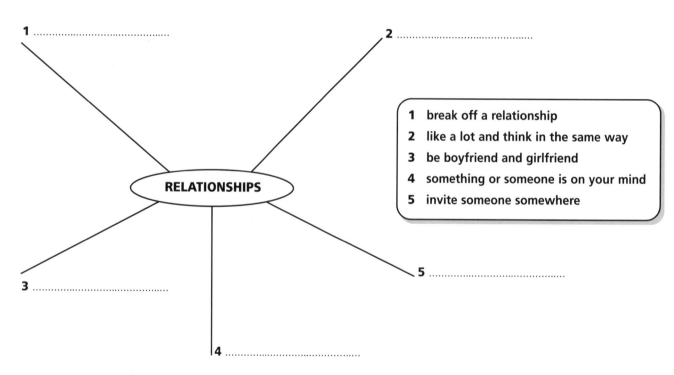

1 ....

2 ....

RELATIONSHIPS

1   break off a relationship
2   like a lot and think in the same way
3   be boyfriend and girlfriend
4   something or someone is on your mind
5   invite someone somewhere

3 ....

4 ....

5 ....

Write your own sentences with the phrasal verbs.

1   ....

2   ....

3   ....

4   ....

5   ....

4 **Now write a reply to one of the problem page letters.**

19 **Stress**

1 **Which of these things stress you?**

parents ☐   school ☐

boyfriends/girlfriends ☐   clothes ☐

money ☐   teachers ☐

brothers and sisters ☐   homework ☐

world news ☐   computers ☐

the weather ☐   mobile phones ☐

2 **The Maharishi school in the USA specialises in making sure that its students don't become too stressed. Listen to Lisa and Steven talking about stress in their lives and then choose the correct ending to each sentence.**

1 Lisa is not stressed …
  a) when she is on holiday.
  b) by much, she thinks she's quite relaxed.
  c) by exams.

2 Lisa is given …
  a) a lot of assignments by her school.
  b) a lot of help with her schoolwork by her brothers and sisters.
  c) a lot of attention because her parents are divorced.

3 Lisa's mother stresses her because …
  a) she doesn't let her go out at weekends.
  b) she expects her to do well in her exams.
  c) she worries about her so much.

4 All Lisa's brother and sisters …
  a) are at university.
  b) are younger and Lisa has to look after them a lot.
  c) are very calm.

5 Lisa is scared of …
  a) the dark.
  b) speaking in public.
  c) letting her mother down.

6 Steven is doing his exams soon but …
  a) he hasn't revised.
  b) he's on a running team and has a part time job at weekends.
  c) he's not worried.

7 Steven thinks that the Maharishi School is …
  a) too hippyish.
  b) not necessary for kids.
  c) a good idea.

8 Steven thinks that his teachers …
  a) only care about their own subject.
  b) are fantastic.
  c) dislike him.

9 Both Steven and Lisa think …
  a) that their classmates would love to go to the Maharishi School.
  b) that their classmates would hate to go to the Maharishi School.
  c) that their classmates would be embarrassed to do yoga at school at first.

3 **Listen again and complete the tables with words from the recording.**

adjective	noun
	ambition
	relaxation
	pride
stressful	
	sympathy
	embarrassment

verb	noun
	imagination
	agreement
	trainer
	feeling
	expectation
	studies

4 **Think of five adjectives to describe your ideal school and five adjectives to describe your ideal teacher. Show your partner. Choose the best three adjectives for your ideal school and the best three for your ideal teacher. Report back to the class.**

20 Internet Nerds

1 You have two minutes to write down all the words you know connected to Internet.

2 Listen to the conversation between Kate and Duncan talking about starting an internet business. Tick the statements that are true.

Statements	True
1 Kate read about a boy who had started in an internet company.	
2 Duncan wants to start an internet company.	
3 Kate wants to start an internet company.	
4 Duncan's company will provide a list of suppliers for the customer.	
5 Duncan says his idea is very simple.	
6 Duncan says his idea is very complicated.	
7 Duncan thinks that the best name is English food.com.	
8 Kate makes suggestions for the name of the company.	
9 Duncan tells Kate she can be the marketing director.	
10 They are going to borrow money from the bank.	

3 Write the words you hear.

....

Now match them with their pronunciation. Then check the spelling.

Write the words you hear.	Pronunciation
1	**a)** /bɪznɪs/
2	**b)** /mærɪd/
3	**c)** /rɪlækst/
4	**d)** /sændwɪdʒɪs/

4 Confusing words. Read this section of the dialogue:

Kate: But Duncan … how will you get the money to start your internet company?

Duncan: I'll have to <u>borrow</u> it. I'll make an appointment to see a venture capitalist. Maybe my Dad will <u>lend</u> me some money as well.

Look at these sentences and complete them with the correct form of *borrow* or *lend*.

a) Can I .... your mobile to quickly phone my mum, please?

b) Did you .... Sarah your bike yesterday?

c) You can't .... that book from the library – you have to read it here.

d) Have you ever .... anyone any money?

e) If you .... me your Linkin Park CD, I'll .... you my Slipknot CD.

f) Why did you .... Steve's jumper – you've got plenty of your own.

5 Work in pairs. Think of a name for Duncan's new company. Write an advert giving customers information about it.

21 Australia

1 How much do you know about Australia? Write down three facts then compare them with a partner.

2 Listen to people describing things in connection with Australia and match them to what is being described.

Number one	*immigrants*
Number two	*Ayers Rock*
Number three	*convicts*
Number four	*surfing*
Number five	*Aborigine*
Number six	*Great Barrier Reef*
Number seven	*Sydney*
Number eight	*The Outback*

3 Choose the correct ending to the sentences.

1 Oliver likes Bondi Beach because...
 a) it's trendy.
 b) it's cool and everyone has really fit bodies.
 c) it's full of nightlife.

2 The only thing Oliver doesn't like about Bondi Beach is...
 a) there are too many surfers in the water.
 b) there are too many tourists.
 c) there are sharks and a dangerous current.

3 Alexis enjoyed...
 a) going to the beach.
 b) the wildlife.
 c) riding camels across the desert.

4 Steven enjoyed...
 a) bungee jumping.
 b) driving across the Outback.
 c) doing a hot air balloon ride at dawn.

5 Steven didn't enjoy...
 a) being bitten by mosquitoes.
 b) the Outback because it was empty.
 c) the heat, it was too much for him.

4 Imagine a British person is visiting your country. What three things would they really like and what would they not like?

Work in pairs. One of you is the British tourist. Ask him / her what they think of your country.

22 Holiday Romance

1 **What do these expressions with 'love' mean? Choose the correct answer.**

1 puppy love ☐
  a) a love of little dogs
  b) two very young people in love

2 cupboard love ☐
  a) a display of affection because you want something
  b) a love of food

3 no love lost between those two people ☐
  a) two people adore each other
  b) two people dislike each other a lot

4 love is blind ☐
  a) when you are in love you can't see what is obvious
  b) if you fall in love, you need glasses

5 love-birds ☐
  a) birds which love each other
  b) two people very much in love

6 not for love or money ☐
  a) you won't do something even if someone begs you to
  b) you can't get what you want no matter how much you pay

2 **(2/4)** **Look at the pictures before you listen to Mel telling Asif about a holiday romance she had. While you listen, put the pictures in the order that they appear in the story. Write a number from 1-6 beside each picture.**

a ☐

b ☐

c ☐

d ☐

e ☐

f ☐

3 **(2/5)** **Dictation. Listen to the sentences describing Mel's holiday romance. Do not write while you are listening. You will have to remember them. You may have to listen more than twice. Each line represents one letter of one word.**

1 *We* ___ ___ ___ ___ ___ ___ ___ *cottage.*

2 *He* ___ ___ ' ___ ___ *me* ___ ___ ___ *the* ___ ___ .

3 *We* ___ ___ *day* ___ ___ ___ .

4 *I* ___ ___ ___ ___ ___ ___ .

5 *He'd* ___ ___ *a* ___ *and* ___ *me a shell.*

6 ___ ___ ___ *me.*

7 *I* ___ ___ ___ , ___ ___ *never* ___ ___ .

4 **Imagine that a friend invites Mel to a Christmas party. At the party, she sees the boy she fell in love with in the summer. What happens? Write the story.**

23 What would you do?

1 Which of these things would you refuse to eat? Is there anything else you refuse to eat?

2 Mel, Asif and Tom are talking about what they would do in different situations. Listen once and tick the adjectives Mel uses when she's talking about Tom.

kind ☐   fashionable ☐   cool ☐   individual ☐

crazy ☐   stupid ☐   lovely ☐   disgusting ☐

3 Who said it? Listen again and tick the correct speakers. Remember, they may not have used exactly the same words.

Sentences 1-4: The handbag incident

Sentences 5-8: The black pudding incident

	Mel	Asif	Tom
a) I'd phone the police.			
b) I chased the boy.			
c) That was stupid.			
d) I think Mel did a good thing.			
e) I'd say I'm not eating that rubbish.			
f) I'd say I don't eat meat.			
g) I'd say I didn't feel well and eat when I got home.			
h) I'd eat it all.			

4 Work in pairs. What would you do in these situations?

  a) Somebody you know tells you that he is going to steal some sweets and chocolate from a local shop. He asks you to go with him. What would you say?

  b) You are with a group of friends. They are all smoking. What would you do?

  c) You see a five-year-old child by herself in a shopping centre. She is crying. What would you do?

  d) You are on a crowded train. You see a pickpocket steal a wallet from a passenger. What would you do?

  e) Your friend has tickets to go to see your favourite band on Saturday. The tickets are free because she won them in a competition. You would love to go but it is your grandmother's 90th birthday and she's having a big family party. What would you do?

  f) You know that a new boy at school is being bullied. What would you do?

  g) All your friends are going to a disco on Saturday night. Your parents have refused to let you go. What would you do?

24 **Addictions**

1 You have two minutes to write down different things people are addicted to.

2 (2/7) Listen to the conversation that Duncan, Kate and Mel had about addictions in British society and answer the following questions.

1 What is Duncan's opinion about alcohol in British society?
   a) Women in Britain don't drink enough alcohol.
   b) British people don't use alcohol well.
   c) Men can drink more alcohol than women.

2 Why does Kate think that the situation might change?
   a) Because the pubs are going to start closing earlier.
   b) Because the pubs are open later and people will be more sensible about drinking.
   c) Because there is a new government.

3 If Mel's friends are too young to buy alcohol in the shops what do they do?
   a) They steal it from other people.
   b) They don't drink anything.
   c) Other people buy it for them.

4 Why does Kate think it's a good idea to legalise drugs?
   a) Because she thinks everyone should have a choice.
   b) Because addicts would get help more easily.
   c) Because she thinks that then no one would take them.

5 What does Duncan say about taking drugs?
   a) More people would try drugs if they were legal.
   b) Lots of people try heroin and then give it up.
   c) Heroin is easier to give up than cigarettes.

3 (2/8) Listen to Duncan saying ten words from the discussion and decide how many syllables they have. The first one has been done for you.

These are the words you will hear:
drinking, criticised, advertisement, later, wanted, difficult, closed, addicted, opinion, understanding

☐ 1	☐ ☐ 2	☐ ☐ ☐ 3	☐ ☐ ☐ ☐ 4
	drinking		

4 Read the two examples of prepositions used in the recording. Complete each sentence with a preposition from the box.

*They are always criticised **for** drinking.*
*Some people are addicted **to** drugs.*

of   of   of
for   for   at   to
from

a) His girlfriend was very jealous .... his friends.

b) She is better .... art than I am.

c) Some young people are not ready .... go to university.

d) His parents were not aware .... his drinking and smoking.

e) Britain is famous .... food such as fish and chips.

f) He was sorry .... the trouble he had caused.

g) How many students are absent .... college today?

h) The jury found him guilty .... drug dealing.

5 **Here is a statement from the discussion:**

If drugs were legalised, a lot more people would take them.

Here are some expressions of agreeing and disagreeing from the discussion. Practise saying them.

Disagreeing: *I don't think it is. In my opinion …*

I don't agree with you, Kate.

Strong disagreement: *Rubbish!*

Agreement: *I think Duncan's right.*

Here are some other expressions:

Strong agreement	*Absolutely!* *Exactly!* *I couldn't agree more.*
Agreement	*You're right.* *I know.* *I agree.*
Agreement but not strong	*I suppose so.*
Polite disagreement	*I see your point, but …* *I'm not so sure.* *Yes, but …* *But don't you think …?*
Strong disagreement	*That's not true.* *You must be joking.* *I don't think that's right.*

Use the expressions to give your own opinion on the statement from the discussion.

6 **Here are some more statements for you to discuss.**

People should not be allowed to smoke in public places.

People who sell drugs should be sent to prison, but people who take drugs shouldn't.

People who drink and drive should have their driving licences taken away.

In Britain, young people aren't allowed to buy alcohol until they are 18. This is a good idea.

25 **Parents!**

1 **Work in pairs and discuss.**

Do you argue with your parents? Do your parents tell you what to do all the time?

Do your parents check up on what you are doing? Do you think your parents treat you fairly?

2 🎧 **Listen to the dialogue between Duncan and Tom and tick the things that Tom doesn't like about living with his parents.**

a) His mum is always saying his hair is too long or too short. ☐

b) His mum wants to borrow his CDs all the time. ☐

c) His dad is always saying his clothes are boring. ☐

d) His mum always wants to tale him shopping for clothes. ☐

e) His dad is always asking him to help with the cooking. ☐

f) His mum lets his sisters do what they want. ☐

g) His mum is always asking him to hoover and do the washing-up. ☐

h) His dad is always laughing at him. ☐

i) His dad is always asking him about his girlfriends. ☐

j) His dad is always giving him advice about his studies. ☐

3 🎧 **Tick the sentences that you hear.**

1 a) Every night they go on at me for playing my music too loud. ☐

   b) Every night they go at me for playing my music too loud. ☐

2 a) I wish my mum would let me make my own decisions. ☐

   b) I wish my mum will let me make my own decisions. ☐

3 a) If I wanted her advice, I'd have asked her about it before. ☐

   b) If I wanted her advice, I'd have asked her for it before. ☐

4 a) She probably doesn't realise she's upsetting you. ☐

   b) She probably doesn't realise she's upset you. ☐

5 a) You shouldn't say things like that to your mum. ☐

   b) You shouldn't have said that to your mum. ☐

4 **Sally is telling her friend, Laura, about her twin sister. She isn't happy with her. Look at the pictures. What is Sally is saying?**

That's my jumper!

That's mine!

a) *She's always borrowing my clothes. I wish she wouldn't.*

b) ....

....

Sally hasn't tidied her room.

You shouldn't eat that.

c ....

d ....

That's my homework.

e ....

f ....

5 **Read this extract from the conversation and answer the questions.**

Duncan: Maybe your dad wishes he had studied harder when he was at school.

Did Tom's dad study hard?

Is he at school now?

Is he happy about the work he did at school?

Read these situations and write what the different people wish.

a) Tom stayed at home and watched a video while all his friends went to a party and had a great time.
        Tom wishes he had gone to the party.

b) Lucy paid £15.99 for her new CD in Brown's. She saw the same CD for £12.99 in Freeman's.
        ....

c) Chris ate a whole chocolate cake and now doesn't feel very well.
        ....

d) While Liz was ice-skating, she fell and broke her arm.
        ....

e) Ed took the bus to town instead of cycling. His wallet was stolen while he was on the bus.
        ....

f) Oliver was taking the dog for a walk when he saw his girlfriend kissing another boy from school.
        ....

6 **Work in pairs. Give Lucy, Ed and Oliver some advice.**

Lucy: ....

Ed: ....

Oliver: ....

26 **Teenage Crime**

1 **Work in pairs and discuss.**

What punishment should the following people get?

a) A ten-year-old child who has committed 8 burglaries in six months.

b) A thirteen-year-old girl who has been caught shoplifting. She stole a jumper.

c) A fifteen-year-old boy who went joy riding and killed an innocent pedestrian.

d) An eighteen-year-old boy who mugged an eighty year old woman.

2 🔊 **Listen to part of a radio talk show where Professor Louise Green is talking about teenage crime. What solution are they using in the US?**

3 🔊 **Read the text below before you listen to the dialogue again. Then listen and fill in the gaps. Note: this is NOT a complete transcript of the conversation.**

Presenter: Professor Green is British, but she has worked at universities **(1)** .... America. Professor, is this a desperate situation?

Professor: It certainly is a big problem. In the States, over **(2)** .... million kids under 18 are responsible for serious violent crime every year. The figure is much bigger if you include non-violent crime.

Presenter: What kind of crimes do teenagers usually commit?

Professor: There are many. Shoplifting, mugging, arson, vandalism, rape and **(3)** ....

Presenter: What can be done?

Professor: If a teenager is happy and communicates well, then he or she probably won't get into serious **(4)** .... The problems start when the kids stop communicating.

Presenter: Are there any other signs?

Professor: If, for example, a child is into violent games or is cruel to pets, parents and teachers may worry. Perhaps they have an interest in **(5)** ....

Presenter: So how can we prevent them from committing serious crimes when they are away from us?

Professor: Some people think that **(6)** .... life in jail can help kids have a better idea of the consequences of crime. They don't go to a real jail but a boot camp.

Presenter: How do boot camps work?

Professor: Life is very hard and kids learn about the **(7)** .... of prison life. Kids hate boot camps and this is important. Basically it's a big **(8)** .... for them.

4 🎧 **2/12 Listen to the sentences and tick the one that you hear.**

1 **a)** We saw a boy stealing a handbag from an old lady. ☐

   b) We saw a boy steal a handbag from an old lady. ☐

2 **a)** I'll probably call the police. ☐

   b) I'd probably call the police. ☐

3 **a)** Teenagers who are happy at home or at school probably won't get into crime. ☐

   b) Teenagers who are happy at home or school probably won't get into crime. ☐

4 **a)** Kids who sometimes get into trouble at school learn from boot camps. ☐

   b) Kids who sometimes get into trouble at school can learn from boot camps. ☐

5 **Read this information about boot camps. Do you think the statements are true or false? Work in pairs to discuss. Write T or F.**

   a) Some parents send their children to boot camp because they are worried they might commit a crime, not because they have committed one. ....

   b) Children can wear what they want in boot camp. ....

   c) They are allowed to talk to their friends. ....

   d) They sleep in tents. ....

   e) They get a choice of food. ....

   f) They have to clean the kitchens and other boring tasks while they are there. ....

   g) They get lectures from ex-offenders. ....

   h) Most children are sad to leave. ....

6 **Write the verbs in brackets in the present perfect simple or continuous.**

   a) Robbie .... ten crimes in the last year. (commit)

   b) He .... the last three weeks in prison. (spend)

   c) His friend .... from the police since Robbie was caught. (hide)

   d) He .... in a forest and he .... food from farmhouses. (sleep; steal)

   e) Robbie .... the police who his friend is. (not tell)

   f) The police .... Robbie six times. (question)

   g) Robbie .... some interesting people in prison. (meet)

   h) They .... him lots of new skills! (teach)

7 **Work in pairs and discuss: How effective do you think boot camps would be in your country?**

> I think they would be ...

> I'm not sure if they would be effective ...

> They definitely wouldn't work because ...

27 Advertising

1 Look at the three items below. What adjectives would you expect to hear in adverts for these items? Write down three for each item.

drink		mobile phone		trainers	
	☐		☐		☐
	☐		☐		☐
	☐		☐		☐

🎧 **Now listen to the adverts and tick your adjectives if you heard them.**

2 🎧 **Listen to the three adverts again and choose the correct options.**

Advert 1

1 Brian couldn't .... but Tony could.
   a) get the girls
   b) stand girls

2 Brian could never get picked for .... but Tony could.
   a) the school play
   b) the team

3 Brian was never .... but Tony was.
   a) the star of English class
   b) good at exams

4 Tony was a success because ....
   a) he drank Cowboy Cola.
   b) he wore Cowboy jeans.

Advert 2

5 Julie's mobile phone cost ....
   a) nothing.
   b) a fortune.

6 Julie gets .... hours of free calls during the week.
   a) three
   b) two

7 During the week, Julie can make her free phone calls ....
   a) during the evening only (after 6 p.m.).
   b) during the day and night.

8 At weekends ....
   a) Julie can make free phone calls all the time.
   b) Julie makes calls to France.

9 Text messages cost ....
   a) ten pence each.
   b) six pence each.

Advert 3

10 Frank is .... the Picasso.
   a) confused by
   b) not very interested in

11 Frank is .... the cost of the Ming vases.
   a) amazed at
   b) bored by

12 Both Frank and his friend think Borange trainers are ....
   a) boring.
   b) amazing.

3 *-ing* or *-ed*? Choose the correct adjective to complete the sentences.

   a) Brian felt ...*depressed*... *(depressed / depressing)* – Brian's assignment was ...*amazing*...
     (amazed / amazing).

   b) I thought that film was extremely .... *(excited / exciting)* with ....
     (fascinated / fascinating) special effects.

   c) How can you possibly find fishing .... *(interested / interesting)*?

   d) Tony looked very .... *(worried / worrying)* when I saw him – his exams are not going well.

   e) I asked the physics teacher to help me with an exercise but it's all so .... *(confused / confusing)*
     that I don't think I'll ever understand it.

   f) I had a really .... *(bored / boring)* weekend and now I just feel .... *(tired / tiring)*
     rather than .... *(relaxed / relaxing)*.

4 **Work in pairs. Tell your partner about your favourite TV or radio advert at the moment. Why do you like it?**

5 **Work in small groups. Choose one of the pictures and write your own advert. Give the product a name and let the customers know why they should buy it.**

28 **The Lost Boy**

1 a) **Read the title of the story and look at the picture. What do you think the story might be about?**

b) **Now read the words in the box in exercise 2. Do you want to change anything about your story?**

2 (2/14) **Read the words in the box. Listen to the story and write each one under one of the characters in the story.**

	cruel caring hungry concerned drunk upset scared kind liar unloving thoughtful ashamed

Dave	Dave's mother	Mark

3 (2/14) **Listen to the story again and write T (true) or F (false) after each statement.**

a) Dave lives with both his parents. ....

b) He is an only child. ....

c) He sleeps in the attic. ....

d) His mother shouted at him and told him to leave home. ....

e) He went to a restaurant. ....

f) He took some money. ....

g) He wanted to play a game of pool. ....

h) He bought a drink. ....

i) Dave had cuts and bruises on him. ....

j) Mark was a policeman. ....

k) Mark made him a pizza. ....

l) Dave's mother came to find him. ....

m) Dave has a bicycle. ....

4 Act out the following in a group.

Mother: Get out! Get out of my house! I don't like you! I don't want you! I never loved you! Get out of my house!

Narrator: Dave finally decides to run for it, hoping his mother won't find him. He is so angry that he walks into a bar and steals a quarter off the pool table.

Mark: What are you doing here? Why'd you steal that quarter?

Narrator: Dave doesn't speak.

Mark: Hey, man. I asked you a question.

Dave: I didn't steal anything. I … I just thought that … I mean, I just saw the quarter and … I …

Mark: First off I saw you steal the quarter, and secondly those guys need it to play pool. Besides man, what are you going to do with a quarter anyway?

Dave: Food. All I wanted was to buy a piece of pizza! Okay?

Mark: *[laughing]* A piece of pizza? Man, where are you from … Mars?

Narrator: Dave doesn't know what to say.

Mark: Hey man, calm down. Here, pull up a stool. Jerry, give me a Coke. Hey kid, are you all right?

Narrator: Dave knows he's not all right.

Mark: Here, drink up. [pause] Hey kid, what's your name? You got a home? Where do you live?

Narrator: Dave acts as if he didn't hear Mark's question.

Mark: You want to tell me what's wrong?

Dave: Mother and I don't get along. She, ah, she, ah … told me to leave.

Mark: Don't you think she's worried about you?

Dave: Right! Are you kidding? I gotta go.

Mark: Where ya going?

Dave: Uhm, I just gotta go, sir.

Mark: Did your mother really tell you to leave?

Narrator: Dave nods.

Mark: I bet she's real worried about you. I tell you what, you give me her number and I'll give her a call. Okay?

Narrator: Dave thinks of leaving, he looks for the exit frantically.

Mark: Come on now, I'm making you a pizza with the works!

Dave: Really? But I don't have any …

Mark: Hey man, don't worry about it, just wait here.

Narrator: Dave's mouth begins to water. He can see himself eating a hot meal. From the front door, a policeman in a dark blue uniform enters. The two men talk for a while, then Mark points to Dave. Dave knows the policeman has come to get him.

Policeman: Don't worry, you're gonna be all right.

5 How would you like the story to finish from here? Work in pairs and write a summary of the ending.

6 British English and American English sometimes use different words and expressions. Explain these three which you heard in the story. How would they be said in British English?

a) soda   **b)** garbage can   **c)** It figures.

Rewrite these American English sentences in British English. You need only change the underlined words.

a) We <u>stood in line</u> to buy some <u>candy</u>.

b) I asked the waitress where the <u>restroom</u> was.

c) Have you had a <u>vacation</u> yet this year?

d) The thieves <u>trashed</u> our house when they broke in last week.

29 **The Environment**

1 **a) Which of these things can be recycled?**

plastic ☐ car batteries ☐ bottles ☐ aluminium ☐ tyres ☐

computer printer cartridges ☐ paper ☐ cardboard ☐ phone books ☐ clothes ☐

b) How can you reuse the following things.

empty jars: ....

empty bottles: ....

plastic bags: ....

old paper and envelopes: ....

old egg cartons: ....

old cans: ....

old yoghurt pots: ....

2 **Listen carefully to Rebecca and Stephen's opinions about the environment.**

Imagine you are Rebecca. What would you say in reply to these statements?

a) Teenagers are too lazy to pick up litter.

b) Factories and business cause most pollution.

c) It wouldn't be fair if people were fined for failing to recycle rubbish.

Imagine you are Stephen. What would you say in reply to these statements?

d) If we don't do something about pollution, we will destroy the planet.

e) You don't have to worry about things that won't happen in your lifetime.

3 **Write the verb in the correct tense – present perfect simple or continuous.**

a) Nut allergies _have been increasing_. People ...._have linked_........... this to pollution. (increase, link)

b) We .... about the environment in our English class this week. (talk)

c) That factory .... the river for months. (pollute)

d) I .... bottles and cans for quite a few years. (recycle)

e) The council .... of five new ways to encourage people to recycle. (think)

f) We .... slowly .... our environment. We ....
about the future at all. (destroy, not think)

g) More and more children .... from asthma in recent years. The air
.... worse and worse in the last twenty years. (suffer, get)

h) Some people .... anything to be recycled. (never take)

4 **Work in pairs or small groups. How would you persuade people to recycle more?
Which of the ideas below would you use?**

posters ☐ advertisements in newspapers ☐ bottle banks near supermarkets ☐

educating primary school children ☐ fine people who do not recycle ☐

30 Growing up in the USA

1 Work in pairs. Would you like to live in a big city or a very small town? Choose one and complete the grid below.

I'd like to live in a	
Advantages	**Disadvantages**

2 Listen to Rebecca talking about where she grew up in the USA.

1 Tick the things which are true about Pleasantville, according to Rebecca.

a) It was a big town. ☐

b) It was a small town. ☐

c) It was near New York City. ☐

d) It was near San Francisco. ☐

e) It was progressive. ☐

f) It was conservative. ☐

g) People liked it because it was busy. ☐

h) People liked it because it was quiet. ☐

i) There were lots of jobs there. ☐

j) Most of the inhabitants travelled into the city each day. ☐

2 Why did Rebecca spend a lot of time with her grandmother when she was a child?

....

3 What activities does Rebecca remember doing with her grandmother?

a) ....

b) ....

4 What are Ila's two best memories?

a) ....

b) ....

5 Which two activities did Nancy do with her friends at school?

a) ....

b) ....

6 How many best friends did Nancy have?

a) one or two ☐   **b)** two or three ☐

c) three or four ☐

7 Which of the three girls was an only child?

a) Nancy ☐   **b)** Ila ☐   **c)** Rebecca

8 Which actual word does Rebecca use to describe herself?

a) shy ☐   **b)** outgoing ☐   **c)** happy ☐

d) angry ☐   **e)** lonely ☐   **f)** funny ☐

9 What does this word mean?

Someone who ....

10 Rebecca thinks her behaviour was

a) typical for an only child. ☐

b) unusual for an only child. ☐

3 Listen and complete these questions. Work in pairs, ask and answer the questions.

a) Where did ....? Can you tell .... it?

b) What's your .... of .... young?

c) Were you the .... who .... or were you a ....?

d) Were you ....? How would ....?

4 Work in pairs. Discuss.
Being an only child is preferable to having brothers and sisters who you argue with all the time.

31 **Humour**

1 **Here are some jokes. Match the two halves.**

1 Why was the thirsty alien hanging around the computer?   **a)** Because 7 – 8 – 9.

2 What's orange and sounds like a parrot?   **b)** One sells watches and the other watches cells.

3 Why is six scared of seven?   **c)** No, they've always been blue.

4 Why did the robber take a bath?   **d)** He was looking for the space bar.

5 What's the difference between a jeweller and a jailor?   **e)** A carrot.

6 Have your eyes ever been checked?   **f)** Because he wanted to make a clean getaway.

2 **Listen and write the answers.**

1 Rebecca thinks it's important not only to

  a) ....

  but also to

  b) ....

2 Would Rebecca ever go out with someone who didn't share the same sense of humour?

  a) yes ☐

  b) no ☐

3 What is important to Rebecca about the person she goes out with?

  It's important that they ....

4 How does Rebecca describe English and American humour? Write E (English) or A (American) next to the words and phrases. (Some words are not used at all by her so leave them blank.)

  a) funny ☐   **f)** loud ☐

  b) silly ☐   **g)** giggle ☐

  c) practical ☐   **h)** intellectual ☐

  d) laugh-out-loud ☐   **i)** childish ☐

  e) dry ☐   **j)** ironic ☐

5 Rebecca says that a certain kind of humour makes her laugh. What is it?

  a) claptrick ☐

  b) slapstick ☐

  c) fat stick ☐

  d) fast trick ☐

  e) elastic ☐

6 Which people do you think are good at this kind of humour?

  a) cabaret artists ☐

  b) clowns ☐

  c) children ☐

7 Nancy uses two words to mean 'stupid'. What are they?

  a) ....

  b) ....

8 Give an example of something which makes Ila laugh.

  If somebody ....

3 Work in pairs. What makes you laugh? Do you laugh at other people's misfortunes? Do you like watching comedy films? Discuss.

4 🔊 A word game. The speaker chooses a topic to talk about from below. Then they get a piece of paper with a mystery word on it, like 'umbrella' or 'helicopter'. They have 20 seconds to talk about the topic on the card, but somewhere they must use the mystery word. If the listeners guess the mystery word, they win a point.

Listen to Ila and Rebecca playing.

5 Now you play the game.

my family	school	holidays
my birthday	music	sport
television	magazines	fashion
my best friend	food	mobile phones
an accident	video games	cinema
my home	shopping	discos
books	the beach	radio

32 **Americans Abroad**

1 **Work in pairs. Do you agree with the following saying? What evidence can you give to support your opinion?**

Travel broadens the mind

2 **Listen to Nancy, an American girl, talking about her time abroad and answer the questions.**

1 **What had Nancy been doing in Europe?**

a) working ☐

b) staying with friends ☐

c) studying ☐

2 **Before she travelled abroad, what did Nancy assume about the 'American way of life'?**

....

3 **What phrase does Nancy use to mean 'keep up with modern progress'?**

....

4 **Nancy uses an idiom with part of the body in it to describe how she was viewed in Europe. Which body part is it?**

a) a bad head ☐

b) a red finger ☐

c) a wooden leg ☐

d) a sore thumb ☐

e) a blue nose ☐

5 **How often did foreigners try to adjust and adapt their attitudes to Nancy and her American friend?**

a) not very often ☐

b) often ☐

c) too often ☐

d) not often enough ☐

6 **What were 'easy accommodations'?**

a) having things translated into English ☐

b) having people talk English ☐

c) being able to speak to people in English ☐

7 **How did people react to Nancy's poor attempts at communicating with them?**

a) They were hostile. ☐

b) They laughed. ☐

c) They welcomed them. ☐

8 **Why did Nancy feel she did not communicate with people as much as she wanted?**

a) There was a lack of language. ☐

b) There was a lack of time. ☐

c) There was a lack of opportunity. ☐

9 **Where did Nancy spend most of her time?**

a) by the sea ☐

b) in the countryside ☐

c) in large cities ☐

10 What two words does Nancy use to mean having a high opinion of oneself and not really thinking about other people?

a) .... b) ....

11 What does Nancy think people ought to do at an early age?

a) travel ☐   d) learn languages ☐

b) communicate ☐   e) study ☐

c) make friends ☐

12 What is the American word for 'autumn' which is mentioned?

....

13 What is Nancy planning to do for the next two years?

a) travel ☐

b) study ☐

c) work as a teacher ☐

14 What are the four things she wants to 'get deep into'?

a) .... c) ....

b) .... d) ....

15 What does Nancy think people should get out of?

a) their bottle ☐   c) their battle ☐

b) their bubble ☐   d) their bundle ☐

16 Which phrasal verb does Nancy use to describe being involved?
Choose prepositions from this list:

> out   in   off   up   with   to

caught ....

17 What three things does Nancy think you learn more about when you travel?

a) dreams ☐   f) friends ☐

b) boundaries ☐   g) strengths ☐

c) hopes ☐   h) adventures ☐

d) weaknesses ☐   i) advantages ☐

e) troubles ☐

3 **Nancy uses the idiom 'to stick out like a sore thumb'. It means to stand out because of something strange. Look at these other idioms with parts of the body and match them to their meanings.**

1 He didn't bat an eyelid.   a) He heard what you said but it didn't make any impression.

2 He played it by ear.   b) He said it before I had chance to say it.

3 It went in one ear and out the other.   c) He was unfriendly.

4 He's got a big mouth.   d) He made a mistake when he was speaking. It was because of carelessness.

5 He took the words out of my mouth.   e) He criticised him and shouted at him for a very small mistake.

6 He's got a sweet tooth.   f) He showed no concern or feeling.

7 It was just a slip of the tongue.   g) He is extremely disrespectful.

8 He jumped down his son's throat.   h) He boasts and he speaks a lot, loudly!

9 He has a cheek.   i) He likes cakes, chocolate, ice cream etc.

10 He was very off-hand today.   j) He used his intuition and he improvised.

33 **Childhood**

1 What's your earliest memory of your childhood? Why do you think you can remember it?

2 You are going to hear a story about a young boy and his cart. Look at the pictures and put them in the correct order.

3 Listen again and choose the correct answers – a, b or c.

1 Mrs Branthwaite
a)   killed cats with poison.
b)   often phoned the police.
c)   hated gardening.

2 At the time of the story, Mrs Branthwaite's poppies
a)   were all dead.
b)   hadn't yet flowered.
c)   were flowering.

3 The author's cart was
a)   very fast.
b)   slow.
c)   new.

4 At first, the super-cart was
a)   a great success.
b)   uninteresting.
c)   too big to move.

5 On the second run, they
a)   took some carts away.
b)   kept the super-cart the same.
c)   added to the super-cart.

6 This time the cart was
a)   too fast.
b)   too slow.
c)   just the right speed.

7 After the second run,
a)   all the poppies were ruined.
b)   half the poppies were ruined.
c)   most of the poppies were ruined.

8 Mrs Branthwaite was
a)   in shock.
b)   arrested.
c)   laughing.

4 Imagine Mrs Branthwaite decides to write to the author's parents to complain about their son's behaviour. Write her letter saying what you want the boy to do now.

34 American Culture

1 Write down three things you associate with America. Compare your list with a partner.

2 (2/22) Read the sentences below then listen to Stephen, Becky and Georgina talking about American culture. Find the false statements for each person.

Stephen

a) The USA is very glamorous. ☐

b) British people like hearing American accents. ☐

c) It's rare that films are made in Britain. ☐

d) British people often have a snobby attitude towards Americans. ☐

Becky

e) All of the cool food, clothing and films come from the USA. ☐

f) British people use American entertainment to relax. ☐

g) The 'American dream' that you can have whatever you want is unrealistic. ☐

h) You often don't notice whether a TV programme is American or British. ☐

Georgina

i) American tourists always seem very loud. ☐

j) You don't usually hear strong American accents on TV. ☐

k) American accents in films are probably toned down for the British audience. ☐

3 Match the American English words with the British English words.

American English	British English
1 flashlight	**a)** flat
2 check mark	**b)** crisps
3 sneakers	**c)** note
4 apartment	**d)** torch
5 subway	**e)** holiday
6 wagon (for shopping)	**f)** roundabout
7 bill	**g)** underground
8 soccer	**h)** boot
9 chips	**i)** tick
10 traffic circle	**j)** football
11 trunk	**k)** trolley
12 vacation	**l)** trainers

4 In the recording, Becky spoke about cool films, cool clothing and cool food. What words could be used instead of 'cool'? Write the words in the box in the correct column.

> exciting   fashionable   delicious   scrumptious   dramatic   stylish   mouth-watering   brilliant   trendy   tasty   designer   gripping

films	clothing	food
exciting		

35 **Poetry**

1 Discuss. Do you enjoy reading poetry? Have you ever written any poetry? Is all poetry romantic? Do you think you should study poetry at school?

2 Listen and answer the questions.

1 How many of the three girls occasionally write poetry?

- **a)** one of them ☐
- **b)** two of them ☐
- **c)** all of them ☐

2 Which of the three girls likes a kind of Japanese poetry (haiku) where each poem consists of only three lines?

- **a)** Rebecca ☐
- **b)** Ila ☐
- **c)** Nancy ☐

3 Who is Rebecca's favourite poet?

- **a)** Tennyson ☐
- **b)** Keats ☐
- **c)** T. S. Eliot ☐

4 What does Rebecca think about reading reports about wars in daily newspapers?

- **a)** She thinks it's boring. ☐
- **b)** She thinks it's important. ☐

5 Would Rebecca fight to defend her country?

- **a)** Yes, because

  ....

- **b)** No, because

  ....

6 Would Nancy fight to defend her home and family?

- **a)** Yes ☐
- **b)** No ☐

7 Does Nancy support US foreign policy?

- **a)** always ☐
- **b)** sometimes ☐
- **c)** not always ☐
- **d)** never ☐

8 Nancy use the following phrases. Use your dictionary to find out what they mean.

- **a)** to make a distinction

  ....

- **b)** to support warfare

  ....

- **c)** to take up arms

  ....

- **d)** to wage war

  ....

9 Would Ila ever consider fighting for a cause she didn't believe in?

- **a)** always ☐
- **b)** sometimes ☐
- **c)** not always ☐
- **d)** never ☐

3 Read these two examples from the recording:

I don't believe in killing people.

I don't necessarily agree with that warfare.

Some verbs are followed by prepositions. Write the verbs under the correct preposition. There will be three in each column.

escape   belong   consist   concentrate   apologise   pay   accuse   depend   recover
believe   differ   approve   specialise   hope   search   insist   succeed   object

from	on	of	for	in	to
escape					

Now choose the correct verbs to complete these sentences. Be careful of the tenses.

a) Who does this book ....? Is it yours?

b) I've .... for my key everywhere but I can't find it.

c) You can't .... your work if you've got loud music playing at the same time.

d) Have you ever been .... bullying?

e) Do you .... ghosts?

f) A dangerous criminal has .... prison – contact the police immediately if you see him.

4 (2/24) **Listen to this war poem and fill in the missing words. It is about the Vietnam War.**

─────────────── *GREEN BERET* ───────────────

He was twelve .... old,
and I do not know his ....
The mercenaries took him and his .... ,
whose name I do not know,
one morning upon .... High Plateau.
Green Beret looked .... on the frail boy
with the eyes of a hurt .... and thought,
a good fright will make him ....
He commanded, and the father was taken ....
behind the forest's green ....
'Right, ... , tell us where they are,
tell us where, or your father – ....'
With eyes now bright and filled with ....
the slight boy said ....
'You've got one minute kid,' said Green Beret,
'tell us where, or we kill father,'
and thrust his wrist-watch .... a face all eyes,
the second-hand turning, jerking on its ....
'OK boy, ten seconds to tell us where they are.'
In the last instant the silver hand shattered the ....
and the forest of trees.
'Kill the old .... ,' roared Green Beret
and shots .... out
behind the forest's green wall
and sky and trees and soldiers ....
in silence, and the boy cried ....

Green Beret stood
in silence, as the boy crouched ....
and shook with .... ,
as children do when their father dies.
'Christ,' said one mercenary to Green Beret,
'he didn't know a damn thing
so we killed the old guy for ....'
So they all went away,
Green Beret and his mercenaries.

And the boy knew ....
And he knew everything about them, the caves,
the trails, the hidden .... and the names,
and in the moment that he cried out,
in that same instant,
protected by frail tears
far stronger than any .... of steel,
they passed everywhere
like ....
across the High Plateau.

Ho Thien

5 **Discuss. Do you like this poem? Why/Why not?**

How would you describe the boy?

How would you describe the soldiers?

What does the poet think of war?

36 **Body Piercing**

1 **Work in pairs. Discuss the following questions.**

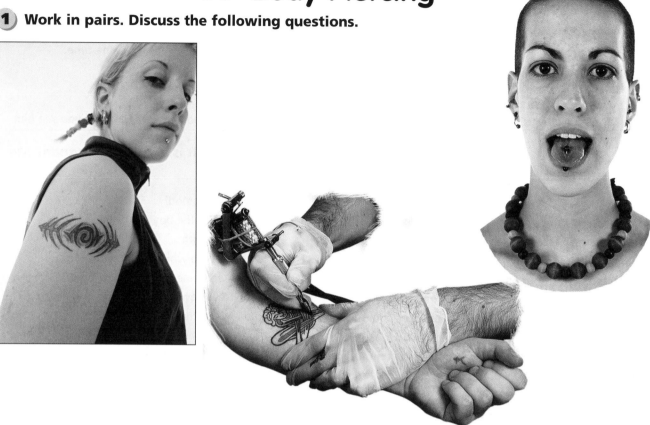

Have you got any piercings or tattoos? How old were you when you got them?
What do your parents think of piercings and tattoos? What do you think of them?

In the UK you have to be 18 before you can have a tattoo. Do you think that is a good idea?

2 **Listen to Becky, Stephen and Georgina talking about body modification and answer the questions.**

Becky

1 How many body piercings has Becky had?

....

2 Why did she think her mum wouldn't mind if she had her nose pierced?

....

3 How does she feel when she sees someone with a lot of tattoos?

....

Stephen

1 Who does Stephen tell us has pierced ears and a pierced eyebrow?

....

2 How does Stephen think society perceives a woman with tattoos?

....

Georgina

1 Why doesn't Georgina wear jewellery?

....

2 What connotations does she think body piercings have?

....

2 **2 26** **Listen to these two questions again. Write the missing words.**

a) What do you .... someone who is ....

....? What's your .... to that?

b) Do you .... if ....

covered in tattoos, ... a man?

4 **Work in pairs. Read this saying and try to explain it.**

Don't judge a book by its cover.

Now answer the questions in exercise 3.

5 **Complete the table with adjectives. They were all in the recording. Listen again if you need to.**

sorrow	
law	
rebellion	
impress	
disgust	
lady	
pain	

Now use the appropriate word from the table in the following sentences.

a) She felt great *sorrow* after the death of her grandmother.

b) Her grandmother always thought it very .... for a woman to swear.

c) I must go to dentist soon – my tooth is really ....

d) You can't buy cigarettes in the UK until you are 16 – it's .... before then.

e) Tony spent ages trying to .... Maria and then found out she already had a boyfriend.

f) I was .... by the way he ate three hamburgers in three minutes.

g) I think there would be a .... in our school if our holidays were shortened.

6 **Complete the sentences from the recording with prepositions.**

a) Mum and Dad weren't too happy .... it.

b) I'd pierced my ears without permission .... my Mum.

c) No one asked for any ID .... me.

d) She congratulated me .... having done such a useful shopping trip.

e) It was my decision to have it done .... the first place.

f) I think it looks good .... some people.

37 **Clubbing**

1 Ask five people in your class the following questions. Can you make any generalisations about your classmates?

What's your favourite activity at the weekend?

....

What do you least like doing at the weekend?

....

Do you go out with your friends or your family at weekends?

....

What time do you have to be home in the evening if you go out with your friends?

....

2 (2/27) Listen to Georgina, Stephen and Becky talking about going to clubs. Make notes about the advantages and disadvantages of going to clubs.

Advantages

Disadvantages

3 (2/27) They mention other things they like to do apart from going to clubs. Listen again and tick the things they mention.

a) going out for a meal ☐ **e)** watching videos ☐

b) going to see a film ☐ **f)** going to a pub ☐

c) going to the theatre ☐ **g)** going to a sports centre ☐

d) going to gigs ☐

4 Read the following expressions from the recording. Then complete them for yourself. Work in pairs and exchange ideas.

a) Sometimes I just feel like ....*staying at home*............ .

b) I do enjoy ....*going to gigs*............ .

c) I go ....*clubbing*............ occasionally.

d) I think it's better to ...*go out with your friends*... .

38 Hooliganism in Britain

1 **What words can 'go with'** *football*. **Find ten in the wordsquare.**

S	T	A	D	I	U	M	P
H	S	T	O	O	B	A	L
O	H	E	M	A	E	T	A
R	I	A	P	I	T	C	H
T	I	K	I	K	O	H	E
S	R	S	H	I	R	T	J
N	A	G	I	L	O	O	H
E	B	P	L	A	Y	E	R

....

....

....

....

....

2 **Listen to Becky, Stephen and Georgina talking about lad culture and hooliganism then finish the sentences.**

a) Stephen thinks that there is a lad culture in Britain ....

b) He thinks that it is just ....

c) Georgina thinks that the lad culture has been created by ....

d) She doesn't think it is representative ....

e) Becky thinks that perhaps young people get obsessed with football because they don't
....

f) Georgina doesn't think football should be a bad thing. The World Cup and the Euro Cup
....

3 **Tick which of the following adjectives describe hooligans in your opinion.**

charming ☐   open-minded ☐   rude ☐   sophisticated ☐   aggressive ☐

polite ☐   intelligent ☐   loud ☐   reserved ☐   fashionable ☐

arrogant ☐   respectful ☐   violent ☐   irresponsible ☐

4 **Discuss the following statements.**

Hooligans should be banned from football matches for life.

Football hooligans should be imprisoned for a minimum of five years.

Football hooligans should have their photographs printed on the front page of newspapers so that everyone knows who they are.

Football hooligans should be made to pay for the damage they cause.

These statements are perhaps extreme. How would you control hooligans?

39 Careers

1 Read the profiles of these students. Which careers would you suggest for them?

> **ANDY:** *artistic, good at maths and geography, interested in the environment, doesn't enjoy languages*

> **PAULA:** *interested in sport, good at science, not a fan of history, likes helping people*

> **SHONA:** *interested in fashion, good at English, likes art, doesn't enjoy science*

> **MARCUS:** enjoys debating, not keen on maths, good at languages, likes being with people

2 (2/29) Listen to Becky, Georgina and Stephen talking about careers, then fill in the gaps in the summaries.

Becky

Becky would like to be a performer. She wants a job where she can use her **a)** .... , perhaps working on the radio or telling **b)** .... on tape. Her dad is **c)** .... and has to take work as it comes, but Becky wants to have a **d)** .... income. If she found a job where she was happy and valued by others, she wouldn't mind that she hadn't achieved the ideal of her **e)** ....

Georgina

Georgina would also like to be a performer, but she knows this career is difficult because her dad is an **f)** .... It's hard for him to make plans or **g)** .... a holiday. There are some terrible **h)** .... ; 97% of actors only earn £4,000 a year through performing. Although she realises she might not be successful, she's going to **i)** .... this career as far as she can. But for now, she's following the advice that adults have always given her – get your **j)** .... first.

Stephen

Stephen would like to be a film director or producer. He doesn't want a job with lots of **k)** .... where people won't notice him. He wants a job that everyone will **l)** .... him by.

3 Ask and answer questions with the following.

> *What are you interested in?*

> *Are you fond of classical music?*

interested in	fed up with
fond of	bored by
keen on	excited about
good at	annoyed with
bad at	impressed by

4 Work in pairs. Write your own profile. Give it to your partner.

Write suggestions of what your partner could do as a career. Give reasons for your choice.

40 **The Internet**

1 **Work in pairs and discuss the following.**

    a) What do you use the Internet for?

    b) Do you have the Internet at home? Does all your family use it?

    c) Do you enjoy using the Internet?

    d) Do you use chatrooms?

    e) Are there any disadvantages to the Internet?

2 **Listen to three teenagers, Stephen, Rebecca and Georgina, talking about the Internet. Who are you like? Tick a box.**

Stephen ☐

Rebecca ☐

Georgina ☐

3 **Listen again then answer the questions.**

    a) Why has Stephen got to cut down on the amount of time he spends on the Internet?

    ....

    b) What is Becky's opinion of the Internet?

    ....

    c) What particular thing does Becky dislike about the Internet?

    ....

    d) What does Georgina think about the safety of Internet chatrooms?

    ....

    e) What has she lied about in Internet chatrooms?

    ....

    f) Why does she lie on the Internet?

    ....

4 **Read the synopsis about 'Sally and the chatroom'. Rewrite the synopsis filling in more detail and then give the story an ending.**

Sally and the chatroom

Sally enjoyed going into chatrooms. She never told anyone her real name or how old she was, she didn't give anyone her address or tell anyone where she went to school.

One day, she had a problem with her parents. They had an argument. She was very unhappy. She went into the chatroom – only Ben was there. She told him what had happened. He said she sounded very sad and asked if she would like to meet up. They could meet in a café in town. Sally agreed.

umbrella	marathon	hot dog
helicopter	tap	hooligan
octopus	sunset	cheek
stopwatch	kettle	top hat
juggler	fountain	handkerchief
peg	novelist	fringe
plug	ornament	goldmine
cello	golf club	jeep
roundabout	rose	owl
toast	injection	comedian

Recording Script

Introduction

The recording script can be photocopied for students. After they have listened, they can underline sections where they have found the answers and confirm they are correct. It can be used to extend vocabulary and also to practise intonation by asking students to read the short dialogues aloud.

★ Students with 2 years of English

1 Making Films

Exercises 2 and 3

Rebecca: Making a movie begins with the scriptwriter and the producer. Sometimes the scriptwriter goes to the producer with the script of a film. Sometimes the producer has a brilliant idea for a film and the producer asks a scriptwriter to write the script.

Stephen: Then, the producer has to find all the other people who work on a film. That's the actors, the director, the photography and lighting people. He or she must persuade people that the film script is good and the film is going to be a big success. Many producers want to persuade famous actors and actresses to act in their films because stars attract big audiences (and big money!).

Farrah: This brings us to another important part of the producer's job. Making a film is very expensive so the producer also has to find some rich people to give the money to pay for everything.

Robin: When they are making the film, the most important person is the director. He or she tells everyone what to do and makes all the important decisions about the film. Some directors like to listen to the opinions of the actors and some directors like to make all the decisions themselves.

Rebecca: When the filming is over, the most important person is the editor. The director usually makes about forty hours of film. But most films are only two hours long. The editor chooses the best parts and puts them all together to make the film that you see in the cinema.

2 How are you Feeling?

Exercise 2

Conversation number one
Robin: Hi Rebecca. How are you?
Rebecca: Not too good actually.
Robin: Oh dear. You do look a bit tired actually. What's the matter?
Rebecca: I'm really exhausted.
Robin: Why?
Rebecca: Oh, I'm studying really hard for my exams, I'm in the school play and I've got a Saturday job.
Robin: You should give something up. Otherwise you'll make yourself ill.

Conversation number two
Farrah: Hi Stephen. How are you?
Stephen: I'm great thanks.
Farrah: You sound very happy.
Stephen: Yes, I'm feeling very excited. I'm going on holiday tomorrow.
Farrah: Oh really? Where are you going?
Stephen: Florida.
Farrah: You lucky thing!
Stephen: Yeah, I can't wait!

Conversation number three
Stephen: Hi Robin. You look cross. What's the matter?
Robin: Oh, I'm really annoyed.
Stephen: Why?
Robin: Anna borrowed my homework and she's left it at home. We have to hand it in today.
Stephen: I don't blame you for being annoyed. What an idiot Anna is!

Conversation number four
Air hostess: Good afternoon Sir. Would you like a …? Oh, you look very pale. Are you all right sir?
Man: Actually, no, I'm not. I'm very frightened. I hate flying.
Air hostess: You really must calm down sir. There is really no reason to be frightened. Flying is very safe. I do it everyday!

Conversation number five
Dad: Hello dear. How are you?
Rebecca: I'm bored.
Dad: Well, if you're bored, why don't you come and help me in the garden?
Rebecca: Dad, I said I'm bored! Gardening is only going to make me more bored.
Dad: Well, why don't you phone Lizzie and go ice-skating then? Here's ten pounds.
Rebecca: Oh thanks Dad. You're the best!

Exercise 3

depressed
confused
interested
worried
excited
frightened
annoyed
bored
relaxed
exhausted

3 Love

Exercise 2

Poem number 1
Roses are red
Violets are blue
Sugar is sweet
And so are you, Stu!

Poem number 2
It was love at first sight
When I saw your face
I can't sleep at night
Without your embrace

Poem number 3
I love coffee
I love tea
I love Robby
Next to me

Poem number 4
My love, I don't mind
That you've stolen my heart
You'll always be mine
Because I love you, Bart

Poem number 5
I love you more than the sun in the sky
I love you more than apple pie
I love you more than a brand-new car
I love you more than a chocolate bar… err maybe not…
But I love you lots!
Marry me, Daniel Potts

Poem number 6
Peter, be my valentine
And everyday I'll feel so fine
Don't say no, please say yes
And I will always do my best

Exercises 4 and 5

Conversation number one
Farrah: Do you like this one?
Rebecca: Oh no. It's too sentimental.
Farrah: What about this one?
Rebecca: Yes. It's all right. Hey, this is a good one. I'm going to send it to Gary.
Farrah: Maybe I'll get the same one for Liam.
Rebecca: That's a good idea.
Farrah: OK, but I need another one.
Rebecca: How many cards are you sending? Here, how about this one with the rabbit on it?
Farrah: Yes, that's sweet.
Rebecca: Good. Let's pay.
Shop assistant: That's £3.25, please.
Farrah: Can we have three first class stamps too, please?
Rebecca: No, just two first class stamps thanks. I'm going to deliver my card by hand.
Shop assistant: There you are. That's £3.77 please.
Rebecca: Thank you. Bye!

Conversation number two
Stephen: Hello.
Flower seller: Hi. Can I help you?
Stephen: Well, I'm not really sure which ones I want.
Flower seller: Are they for your girlfriend on Valentine's Day?
Stephen: Yes, they are.
Flower seller: Well, how about some nice red roses then? Girls love red roses, don't they?
Stephen: Everyone buys red roses on Valentine's Day. I prefer those tulips actually.
Flower seller: All right mate. Whatever you want. How many would you like?
Stephen: Oh, a big bunch please.
Flower seller: Is that all right?
Stephen: Lovely. How much is it?
Flower seller: That's £5, please.
Stephen: Here you are.
Flower seller: Thanks. Have a nice day.
Stephen: Goodbye.

Conversation number three
Dad: It's Valentine's Day tomorrow. I don't know what to buy your mum this year.
Farrah: Flowers? Chocolates?
Dad: I always get her flowers or chocolates. That's boring.
Farrah: Why don't you take her out to a posh restaurant? She'll like that.
Dad: That's a good idea. I think I'll book a table now. She loves Thai food, doesn't she?
Waitress: Hello, Thai restaurant.
Dad: Hello. I'd like to book a table for two for tomorrow night.
Waitress: No problem, Sir. What time would you like to eat?
Dad: 7.30?
Waitress: Yes, that's fine. Would you like smoking or non-smoking?
Dad: Non-smoking please.
Waitress: That's fine. I look forward to seeing you at 7.30.
Dad: Thank you. Goodbye.

Conversation number four
Rebecca: Hi Steven. What are you doing?
Stephen: I'm making a cake.
Rebecca: You're joking. I've never seen you cook anything before.
Stephen: Well, it's for my girlfriend, Katie. It's Valentine's Day tomorrow and she loves chocolate cake.
Rebecca: That's a nice idea. Would you like some help?
Stephen: Yes, please. Could you mix the cocoa powder in with the flour?
Rebecca: Fine. How much do I need?
Stephen: Three tablespoons.

Exercise 6

a) **Farrah:** What about this one?
   Rebecca: Yes. It's all right.

b) **Rebecca:** Here, how about this one with the rabbit on it?
   Farrah: Yes, that's sweet.

c) **Farrah:** Why don't you take her out to a posh restaurant?
   Dad: That's a good idea.

4 Losing Weight

Exercise 2

Interviewer: Hello and welcome to Greenhill Camp.

Alison: Hi.

Interviewer: Please sit down. How are you?

Alison: Fine thanks.

Interviewer: I would like to ask you a few questions about your diet and lifestyle so that we can advise you on the best programme to help you lose weight.

Alison: That's fine.

Interviewer: First of all, I need to fill out your personal details. What's your name?

Alison: Alison Brown.

Interviewer: And how old are you?

Alison: Fifteen.

Interviewer: What's your date of birth?

Alison: The ninth of March, 1985

Interviewer: How often do you exercise? Do you play any sports?

Alison: I do sports at school. That's three hours every week. But that's all. I don't do any sports outside of school.

Interviewer: Do you ever do any cycling or walking?

Alison: Very rarely because my mum takes me to school in the car. I have a bike but I don't ride it very often because there's lot of traffic and pollution in my area.

Interviewer: Did you know that doing jobs around the house like hoovering or gardening can help you lose weight? Do you help your parents in the house?

Alison: Not really. I hate hoovering and gardening. It's so boring.

Interviewer: So, what do you enjoy doing in your spare time?

Alison: I like watching TV or playing computer games.

Interviewer: I see. Now I'd like to ask you a few questions about your diet. Can you tell me what you usually eat for breakfast?

Alison: Well, I'm usually in a hurry so I eat some biscuits or a packet of crisps.

Interviewer: What do you usually eat at lunchtime?

Alison: My friends and I go to the chip shop and buy a large portion of chips.

Interviewer: And what do you eat at home in the evenings?

Alison: I eat fish or chicken with potatoes and vegetables or some pasta. For dessert I eat a piece of fruit or a yoghurt.

Interviewer: Do you often eat snacks between meals?

Alison: Sometimes. I eat a packet of crisps or a chocolate bar during my breaktime and I often eat biscuits when I arrive home from school.

Interviewer: Right. Good. Thank you for your help. I will work out a programme for you and tell you about it tomorrow.

Exercise 3

Interviewer: Well, Alison, you eat too many snacks and you don't do enough exercise. You'd better start walking to school in the morning. You'd better find some hobbies that are more active. If I were you, I'd go cycling in the park at weekends or go ice-skating. Why don't you join an aerobics class if you don't like sport? Help your parents around the house. You'll burn calories and your parents will be pleased. Perhaps they will pay you for doing some jobs. That way, you'll be earning money and losing weight at the same time. You'd better start eating a good breakfast. Cereal and toast is a healthy breakfast. If you eat a healthy breakfast, then you don't need to snack later. You'd better stop eating so many unhealthy foods like crisps and biscuits. If you feel hungry, eat a piece of fruit instead.

5 Video Games

Exercises 2 and 3

Sally: Stephen, what do you think of video games?

Stephen: I like video games because the games are fun even though you don't really learn anything from them. Some of my friends just sit there all day, all weekend and play and I think that's bad. But it's also useful because that's how you make all your friends at school. Everybody always talks about video games.

Sally: Robin, what do you think? Do you agree with Stephen?

Robin: Many people think that video games are a bad influence on children but I disagree. I love football and basketball video games. I also love Grand Theft Auto. In Grand Theft Auto, players get points by stealing cars and killing police officers. Grand Theft Auto doesn't make me want to go out and steal cars. Video games don't influence me.

Sally: What about you Rebecca? Do you like video games?

Rebecca: No, I hate video games. Video games send a bad message to kids. They show you how to steal or shoot a gun. I can't even play for an hour. It gets boring. My brother is so into games that he can't even read a book.

Sally: Farrah, what do you think?

Farrah: It's true that the time you spend playing video games, you might read a book or do homework which could educate you. However, I love video games. Sometimes I play so much that my neck and back start aching from bending over. When I play for a long time my hands get sore, mostly on my thumbs. That's not very good. But video games have some advantages. Playing video games helps your hand-eye co-ordination and they can also help to improve your memory.

6 At the Airport

Exercise 2

As you go into the airport, the check-in desks are on your right and the toilets are on your left. The duty-free shop is next to the toilets. Opposite the entrance there is a bar. The bar is between passport control and the restaurant. There is a newsagent's next to the restaurant. The hat shop is between the newsagent's and the duty-free shop.

Exercise 3

Stephen: You had your bag at the check-in desk. The lady asked you if you wanted to take it as hand luggage and you said yes. So your bag can't be at the check-in desk.

Farrah: Your bag can't be in the newsagent's because you didn't go into the newsagent's.

Robin: Your bag can't be in the toilets because you asked me to hold your bag when you went into the toilets.

Farrah: Your bag can't be in the bar because it is closed today.

Stephen: Your bag can't be in the duty-free shop because when we left the shop I put the perfume in your bag.

7 Helping a Friend with a Problem

Exercise 2

Anna: Is having an eating disorder the same as being on a diet?

Expert: No, having an eating disorder is an illness. Dieting is about losing a little weight in a healthy way.

Anna: What causes an eating disorder like anorexia?

Expert: Nearly all of our patients have low self-esteem. That means they don't think they are good enough as they are. They may even hate themselves.

Anna: What are the symptoms of an eating disorder? What are the signs?

Expert: Well, some of the symptoms are:

- *always thinking about food and the calories in it,*
- *losing a lot of weight very quickly,*
- *trouble sleeping,*
- *feeling cold,*
- *and feeling depressed.*

Anna: How can other people help?

Expert: You cannot make people eat. Do not concentrate on the food. Focus on the emotional problems that are causing the disorder. There are groups you can contact and some very good websites.

Anna: Thank you.

Exercise 3

1) Hey there. You look sad
   Are you feeling all right?
   If you're having problems
   You mustn't be uptight.

2) Everyone has problems
   Famous people do too
   But problems seem smaller
   If they're shared between two.
   Chorus
   A problem shared
   is a problem halved
   If you share your problems
   They get smaller each day
   If you share your problems
   They will soon go away

3) Problems with your parents?
   They tell you what to do
   Write to a problem page
   That'll stop you feeling blue.

4) You love your friend's brother
   Your homework gets you down
   You hate your sister and
   Your parents make you frown.
   (Chorus)

5) Don't worry, be happy
   Ask your friends for advice
   Find a solution and
   Your life will feel so nice.

6) Talk your problems over
   Don't stay at home and cry
   Get a friend to listen
   It's easy if you try.
   (Chorus)

8 New York City

Exercises 2 and 3

Mother: We need to start thinking about what we're going to do in New York. We have to make some bookings. We can do it on the Internet. Do you know what you want to see and where you want to go?

Anna: I want to go to the Statue of Liberty. It's got a really interesting history. You know, all the people who came from other places to start a new life in America. I really like reading about things like that. Maybe we could go on a tour.

George: I don't mind going on a short tour. But I don't like spending a lot of time listening to a tour guide.

Father: Don't worry, we won't spend hours in tours. There's too much to see. I want to go to the Museum of Modern Art.

Mother: Well, I know you don't like shopping but I have to do some shopping.

Father: You'll be able to shop. I'm sure you'll find time!

George: I want to go to the top of one of the tall buildings – like The Empire State Building.

Anna: Great. You can see for miles from there.

Father: And how about a boat trip around the island?

George: What island?

Anna: Manhattan Island, George. Most of New York City is on it!

George: Oh, right.

9 Text and Phone Messages

Exercise 2

1) **Ellie:** Well, I spend about five pounds a week on my phone. I used to use it mainly for calling but now I use it mostly for texting. I always take it with me.

2) **Simon:** I don't have a mobile phone but my mum and dad say that they might give me one for Christmas. They think phones are a good idea because they can get in touch with me wherever I am.

3) **Kate:** My mum is cool about texting. She says that when she was a girl she and her friends used to pass each other notes on paper. They'd pass notes around in the classroom behind the teacher's back. She thinks texting is just a high-tech version of the same thing.

4) **Ms Anderson:** Yes, our school has fairly strict rules about mobiles. Students have to turn them off before going into the classroom – we take them away otherwise. They can turn them on when class is over.

5) **Mr Harrison:** I know some people worry that kids might not learn to spell words properly – that they'll use the short forms of words for text messages. But I don't. I think texting is great – they have to work out ways to write with fewer letters.

Exercise 3

Message 1

Simon: Hi. It's me, Simon. Do you want to go to the football match on Saturday? Give me a ring when you get in. The number is 0208-478961. Thanks.

Message 2

Tom: Hi, this is Dad. I'm at the hotel. Can you ring me before 7:00? The number is 01299-309255. Bye.

Message 3

Anna: Hi. Anna here. Call me as soon as you can. I'm on my mobile. The number is 078-687-6890. Thanks.

Message 4
Ellie: Hello. This is Ellie. I'm going to be late. Please ring me when you get in. The number is 0878-9678998.

Exercise 5

Mobile World
Talking on the phone in this mobile world
No-one's ever home in this mobile world
Everyone's got something to say, make yourself be heard
Say it loud and say it clear, every single word

Chorus
Talk, talk, talk, talk
Here in this crowded room
Talk, talk, talk, talk
Trying to get a message through
Talk, talk, talk, talk
Ring tone plays a tune
Talk, talk, talk, talk
The whole world is calling

On top of a mountain, standing in the snow
You can talk on your mobile wherever you go
The signal may not always be clear
But there's someone out there who would love to hear
(Chorus)
Making contact when you like and never feeling alone
Distance is no problem with a mobile phone
You can text a message, you can use your voice
When you've got a mobile phone, you've got a choice
(Chorus)
All around the world, which seemed so far away
You can get through in seconds, night and day
Talking on the phone, in this mobile world
From Australia to Rome, in this mobile world

10 Schools in Britain

Exercise 2

Sally: Sophie, what kind of school do you attend?
Sophie: I go to a state secondary school in London. It's a large school. I like going to my school because it's quite relaxed. I won a music scholarship to go there. I have extra music lessons.
Sally: That sounds interesting. What instruments can you play?
Sophie: I can play the trumpet, the keyboards, the guitar and the flute. However, it is hard work. I have to complete all my homework and do several hours of music practice every night.
Sally: Do you like your school?
Sophie: Yes, I do. It's relaxed and informal. We don't have to wear a school uniform. We can wear whatever we like.
Sally: That's nice. What about you, Jack?
Jack: I go to a private boys' school which is strict. I hate wearing my school uniform. It's so unfashionable. You even have to wear blue socks. If you are caught wearing red socks, you get a detention.
Sally: Ryan, what about your school? Is it strict or relaxed?
Ryan: Well, I don't have much freedom because I go to a boarding school. However, I don't mind boarding. Sometimes I miss my family but I love living with all my friends. Everyone becomes really good friends and it's a lot of fun. When I'm at home for the holidays, I get bored.
Sally: It sounds fun.

Ryan: Yes, it is. However, there are a lot of stupid rules. Our school has a grading system for bad behaviour. You lose points if your uniform is untidy or dirty, for lateness, for answering back, talking in class or bringing chewing gum to lessons. We are young adults but they treat us like children.
Sally: What about you, Louise? What kind of school do you attend?
Louise: I go to a drama school which is really brilliant. In the mornings we have lessons in dance, acting and music. In the afternoons, we have to study the more usual subjects like maths, English and geography. I enjoy both the mornings and the afternoons. It's important to get good exam results because acting is a very competitive career.
Sally: Jack, you've only told us negative things about your school. Is there anything you enjoy doing at school?
Jack: Yes, there is. My favourite subject is chemistry. Our chemistry teacher, Mrs Lacey, is inspiring. She's always encouraging us to think for ourselves. I love doing experiments in the chemistry lab. But I'm not a swot! I also enjoy playing football with my mates at breaktimes.

Exercise 3

Example:
music: There are 2 syllables in music.
musical: There are 3 syllables in musical.

1) lesson
2) homework
3) uniform
4) strict
5) private
6) detention
7) chemistry
8) experiment
9) behaviour
10) study

Exercise 4

State education is free but some parents pay for private education.
Private schools are very expensive and about 7% of British kids go to them.
Children go to nursery school from three years old to five years old.
They go to primary school when they are five years old.
They start secondary school at 11. Children in the UK must go to school until they are 16 years old.
They can stay at school for two more years until they are 18 years old.
Children at secondary school in Britain have to study ten subjects.
The main subjects are English, mathematics and science.
Children must spend more time studying these subjects.
The other subjects are history, geography, art, one foreign language (French is the most usual), design and technology, physical education and music.
When they are 16 years old, students have to take General Certificate of Secondary Education exams (GCSEs) in as many subjects as they can manage, often about eight or ten.
At 18 they take A levels which qualify them for entry to university. Students in the UK specialise early, choosing just three or four subjects to study at A level.
About 20% of young people go to university or college.

11 Being a Detective

Exercise 2

1) The killer can't have been a woman.
2) The killer must have been here when the victim arrived.
3) The crime can't have happened after 4 o'clock.
4) The murder weapon must have been a gun.
5) The neighbours must have heard the shots.

12 Food

Exercise 2

Sally: Sophie, can you remember what you ate yesterday?

Sophie: What? Everything I ate? Oh dear. This could be embarrassing.

Sally: Yes, everything you ate and drank!

Sophie: Oh gosh, well, for breakfast I had cornflakes with some sugar and milk. I always have cornflakes in the morning because it's quick and easy. At school I had a chicken burger and a bottle of water at lunchtime. Chicken burgers are quite healthy and water is good for your skin. In the afternoon I had a fruit smoothie. A smoothie is a drink made with yoghurt, fruit and ice. It was a banana and strawberry flavoured smoothie. For dinner I had burger, chips and peas. Burger and chips – that's not very healthy, is it?

Sally: What about you, Ryan?

Ryan: I'm not sure if I can remember. My school food is tasty but it gets very boring.

Sally: Oh yes, you go to boarding school so you have to eat school food for every meal. You poor thing!

Ryan: That's right. Let's see. For breakfast I had two slices of white toast with butter, I think, and a glass of orange juice. The orange juice at school isn't freshly squeezed so it's not very nice. For lunch I had chicken curry and rice. It was delicious. I love curry. For dessert I had apple crumble and custard. The school apple crumble is OK, but my mum's apple crumble is better. I drank a glass of water. I drink water every day at school because they don't provide anything else. For supper I had cheese and tomato pizza with a mixed salad, a chocolate mousse and an apple.

Sally: Curry! Chocolate mousse! The food at your school sounds quite sophisticated. What about you Jack? Do you like your school food?

Jack: The school dinners are nice but the portions are small. I've never seen salad on the menu. Fruit is available but I don't eat it because my favourite is chicken and chips and that takes up all my £1.25. That's what I had yesterday. Chicken and chips with ketchup and a can of lemonade. Lemonade is my favourite soft drink and I drink it every day. For breakfast I had Weetabix with milk. My dad always buys Weetabix when he goes shopping. For dinner I had lamb chops with mashed potatoes and carrots, followed by a piece of chocolate cake. My mum makes the best chocolate cake in the world!

Sally: Louise, do you like chocolate cake?

Louise: Of course, I love it. Actually I did eat chocolate cake yesterday because it was my mum's birthday. For breakfast, I had two croissants with butter and jam. Normally, we only have croissants at the weekend but yesterday it was a special treat for my mum's birthday. Unfortunately, school dinners weren't special. I had a tuna sandwich and a bag of crisps. I usually have a sandwich for lunch because the sandwiches at school are quite tasty. In the evening, my dad and I cooked a special dinner for my mum. We had smoked salmon to start with. I love smoked salmon, don't you? Then, we had vegetable lasagne. It was delicious. I made the lasagne. It's very simple to make. Finally, we had birthday cake. It was chocolate cake. We didn't make the cake, we bought it from a shop.

Sophie: Hey, what about you Sally? What did you eat yesterday?

Sally: Well, I didn't eat very healthily even though I'm supposed to be on a diet. I went to a fast food restaurant yesterday with my brother and my two nephews.

Exercise 3

Number 1

Assistant: Hello. Can I help you?

Man: Yes. I'd like some chicken nuggets, please.

Assistant: How many chicken nuggets would you like? Six or twelve?

Man: Six please.

Assistant: Would you like any fries with that?

Man: No thanks.

Assistant: Would you like anything to drink?

Man: Could I have a large coke?

Assistant: OK.

Man: Oh, and I'd like a doughnut please.

Assistant: That's £3.75 please.

Number 2

Assistant: Hello. Can I help you?

Boy: Yes, I'd like a cheeseburger.

Assistant: No problem. Would you like fries with that?

Boy: Yes please.

Assistant: Large or regular?

Boy: Regular.

Assistant: The special Burger meal gives you cheeseburger, fries and a drink for just £2.99. That's very cheap.

Boy: All right. I'll have a Burger meal, please.

Assistant: Which drink would you like?

Boy: Orange juice, please.

Assistant: OK. That's £2.99.

Number three

Assistant: Hello. Can I help you?

Sally: Could I have a veggie burger, please?

Assistant: Would you like any fries with that?

Sally: No thanks. I'm on a diet.

Assistant: Would you like anything to drink?

Sally: Yes. I'd like some water. And a cup of tea, too.

Assistant: Is that everything?

Sally: Yes, thanks.

Assistant: That's £2, please.

Number four
Assistant: Hello. Can I help you?
Boy: Could I have a Big Burger?
Assistant: Would you like any fries with that?
Boy: No thanks. I'd like onion rings
Assistant: Would you like a drink?
Boy: Yes, please. I'd like a coffee.
Assistant: Anything else?
Boy: Umm. I'd like an ice cream, please.
Assistant: What sauce would you like on top?
Boy: What flavours do you have?
Assistant: Chocolate, strawberry or butterscotch.
Boy: Chocolate, please.
Assistant: That's £4.50 please.

Exercise 4
Assistant: Hello. Can I help you?
<beep>
Assistant: Would you like any fries with that?
<beep>
Assistant: Would you like a drink?
<beep>
Assistant: Would you like anything else?
<beep>
Assistant: That's £3.75, please.

13 Black Rights in America

Exercise 2
Louise: I think Muhammad Ali is an inspiring figure. He is one of the most popular figures of the 20th century. He was a great sportsman but he was also very charming and witty. This combination is quite unusual.
Sophie: I detest boxing. It is a mindless, cruel sport. Muhammad Ali was exploited by people who wanted to make money from him. Now, he is a very sick man. But I think he is a hero because of the way that he has dealt with his illness. He is very dignified.
Ryan: I'm a fan of boxing. Muhammad Ali was an amazingly fast and graceful boxer. He is a boxing legend and rightly so.
Jack: Some people didn't like him because he was boastful. But I think Muhammad Ali is a strong person who stands up for what he believes in. He made sacrifices in his career to help the cause of black rights in America. I think this is heroic.

Exercise 3
Louise: Most American blacks originally come from an area in western Africa. This area had efficient governments and a lot of its wealth came from trading. The slave trade began in the early 1500s. For the next 300 years millions of black Africans were taken by ship to the USA and Latin America.
Ryan: During the Revolutionary War in America (from 1775 to 1783) many Americans turned against slavery. They felt it was against human rights. However, in the south of the USA there were large farms which grew cotton, tobacco and other crops. They needed lots of workers and most of their workers were slaves. Most of the people who were against slavery lived in the north of America. This would eventually lead to a civil war between the north and south.

Jack: After the Civil war the US government helped freed slaves to find jobs, houses and education. But as they tried to enter society, many black people found that the racism of white people made life difficult.
Sophie: Gradually the civil rights movement started up. In 1955 Rosa Parks, a civil rights activist, was arrested for disobeying a city law that required blacks to give up their seats on the bus when white people wished to sit in them. Black people protested by refusing to ride on the buses. They protested for 382 days. The protest ended when the city abolished the bus law.
Louise: The most famous civil rights leader was Martin Luther King. He asked African Americans to protest peacefully. During the early 1960s the efforts of the civil rights groups ended discrimination in many public places including restaurants, hotels and cemeteries.

14 Summer Camp

Exercise 2
Summer Camp. Scene 1: In Gemma's house at the start of the summer holidays
Mrs Redwood: Gemma, have you packed everything for the camp?
Gemma: Yes, Mum. I wish you'd stop asking me that!
Mrs Redwood: What about your trainers?
Gemma: I told you! Everything's packed! Anyway, if I forget something, I can buy it in the camp shop.
Mrs Redwood: The camp shop is tiny. They won't sell much there. And it's far away from a supermarket – in fact, it's far away from anywhere...
Mr Redwood: Well, that's a good thing.
Gemma: What do you mean?
Mr Redwood: You know what I mean, Gemma. You'll be far away from Andy. He's a bad influence on you. Since you met Andy your behaviour has changed. You're irritable with us; you don't spend enough time on your school work; you go out at night without telling us what time you'll be home …
Gemma: That's not fair! You don't know Andy. He's a good person.
Mr Redwood: Gemma, we don't want you to see him again. Your mother and I have talked about this, and we feel it's the right thing for you – and for Andy. You are both too young to be serious about each other. You've got your future to think about.
Gemma: You just don't understand! Just leave me alone! I don't want to talk to you!

Scene 2: Later that night at Andy's house
Andy: Calm down, Gemma. Tell me again what they said. Did they actually say you couldn't ever see me again?
Gemma: Yes. They think that it's not going to be a problem because I'm going to summer camp with the youth club tomorrow. The camp is 60 miles away, in the middle of Elsam Forest. It's not near a railway station or a bus route – so we won't be able to see each other for two whole weeks.
Andy: Well, do you want to see me?
Gemma: Of course I do. You know that.

Andy: Well, I've been thinking about this – and here's my plan. Dad's old motorbike is in the garage. I haven't got a licence because I'm too young but I can ride a motorbike. I've ridden it before but Dad won't let me ride it without him. It won't take long on a motorbike.

Gemma: But Andy, what will happen if the police catch you – or if your parents find out?

Andy: Gemma, trust me! I'll be careful. I'll make sure I'm home before they get back from work. When can we meet?

Gemma: Tuesday. I'll have my mobile with me. Ring me when you get to Elsam Forest. I'll meet you at the gate of camp. Oh Andy! I can't wait!

Andy: Neither can I. I'll miss you! See you on Tuesday.

Gemma: Bye! Take care on the bike!

Scene 3: One week later in Elsam Forest. Andy and Gemma are having a picnic in the forest.

Gemma: What a wonderful day! I'm so glad you came, Andy.

Andy: Me too. Two weeks is too long to be away from each other. Come on, let's go for a walk before you have to go back to camp.

Gemma: OK. There's a lake near here, just down this path. Oh no! What was that noise?

Andy: I don't know – we'd better find out! Quick! It sounds like a car crash!

Woman: Help! Help!

Andy: Gemma, have you got your mobile? Quick! Phone for an ambulance.

Gemma: OK, Andy, they're trapped in the car! Get them out before it catches fire!

Andy: It's OK! I'm going to try to pull you out. Can you move your legs?

Man: I think I've broken my ankle – and look at all this blood. My head's bleeding! Don't worry about me. Help my wife!

Andy: We'll get you out. What's your name?

Woman: Susan, and this is my husband, Richard.

Andy: It's OK, Susan. Put your arm around my neck. I'm going to carry you across the grass and I'm going to put my coat around you. Don't move – wait until the ambulance comes.

Woman: Thank goodness you were here!

Andy: Try to stay quiet, the ambulance will be here soon.

Gemma: Andy, the ambulance is on its way. Here, take my jumper. Put it under her head.

Andy: Gemma! Run over to the motorbike. There's a small first aid kit in the back! We can do something about Richard's head.

Man: I don't understand what happened – we've been driving through this forest for years. We've never had an accident before.

Scene 4: Twenty minutes later. The ambulance is driving away. A policeman and a journalist walk over to Andy and Gemma.

Policeman: You did a fantastic job. You saved those people's lives.

Andy: Thank you but it was the only thing to do.

Gemma: We just did what was necessary. It was nothing special.

Chris Coulson: Hi, kids. I'm Chris Coulson. I'm a journalist on the Elsam Gazette. You two are heroes. Can I take your photo?

Andy: What?

Chris Coulson: I want to put your photo in the local paper. Now, is that your motorbike over there? Just go and stand next to it. That'll make a great picture.

Gemma: I'm not allowed to see you! What are we going to do? What will my parents say?

Andy: Yeah! What about my Dad? He'll go mad if he finds out I've taken the motorbike!

Exercise 3

Ending 1

Chris Coulson: Is something wrong?

Andy: Well, we've got a bit of a problem. You see that's my dad's bike and he doesn't know I've borrowed it. If he sees my picture in the paper he'll be angry.

Policeman: Do you actually have a licence?

Andy: Uh, no, I, …

Policeman: I'm sorry, but I must ask you to come with me to the police station.

Ending 2

Andy: Oh, I don't care any more. I'm sure Dad won't mind when he learns I'm a hero. Come on, Gemma. Let's do it!

Gemma: I agree! Now they'll really believe me. You're a good person; you're a hero!

Ending 3

Andy: Please don't be offended, but we're both really shy and we don't think we've done anything special. We don't want any publicity for this.

★★ Students with 2-3 years of English

15 Anna's Story

Exercise 2

Part 1

There is no easy way to tell your children something like that. Obviously there are ways that doctors and social workers suggest but the basic message is the same, 'I am HIV positive'. People say mum should have told us immediately and I shouldn't have found out by accident. Mum was waiting for a good time to tell us. Besides, she was just learning to live with the news herself. She didn't know how we'd cope. She was waiting for a good time. Trouble is, there never was a good time for that sort of news. If we'd won the lottery, I'd married Brad Pitt, we'd all lived in paradise and my brother had got a job at last, it still wouldn't have been a good time. What actually happened was I came home from school. Mum didn't hear me come in. I heard that she was talking on the phone in her bedroom. She does this when it's a call that she doesn't want me or my brother to know about. I could hear her talking about test results, I immediately thought it was my school telling her about the end of term exams. Then I heard her say, SHE needed regular tests. I realised I must be listening to a crucial conversation. Then she said HIV. My brain played it back to me again and again. I was checking it wasn't another phrase. I was trying desperately to convince myself that I had heard wrongly. After a week I really believed I'd imagined it. I didn't ask mum about it because I was scared of the answer. Then two weeks later, she told me and my oldest brother that she needed to have a serious talk with us about something after the younger kids had gone to bed. She was shaking. At about 8 o' clock, my brother said, 'Come on mum, what is it? Don't tell me you are going to let Adam move in again!' Adam is her ex-boyfriend. She just burst into tears but said she wouldn't tell us 'til Hilary – my sensible aunt – her sister arrived. I was hoping Hilary would never arrive because then she wouldn't need to tell us. When I heard the doorbell, I wanted to ignore it. Hilary had come round to help mum tell us. In the end Mum told us very calmly. She'd obviously practised it. When she'd found out the truth about Adam, she'd had a test as a precaution. The test result was HIV positive.

Exercise 3

Part 2

When mum told us, we just sat there. My aunt started giving us some sort of biology lesson, telling us the difference between HIV and AIDS. We didn't need it. We'd learned about it at school. What we weren't prepared for was needing to know about it. With most bad news there's something you can do to change it but this was irreversible. Mum tried to discourage me from thinking like that. She explained about new drugs that are saving thousands of people's lives. After a while I understood that our lives were not going to change so dramatically. Mum wasn't actually ill, she just had the virus. Even so, I really wanted to talk to someone about it. I wanted to talk to Jason, my older brother, but he would change the subject when I mentioned it. So, I spoke to Karen about it. BIG

MISTAKE. Karen can be really both horrible and really nice. We were in her bedroom, playing computer games and Karen was in a bad mood 'cos her mum wouldn't let her go out on Friday night. She suddenly said, 'I wish my mum was more like yours.' I started to cry. She asked what the matter was. I should have lied but instead I told her about mum being HIV positive. She was a good listener and I trusted her. She told me that me and my mum were really brave. She sounded like she really cared. She said I could talk to her any time. I told her not to tell anyone. She said she wouldn't dream of telling anyone. Two days later I was at school. I walked past these two girls. I heard one of them whisper, 'That's her. Her mother's got AIDS.' The entire school seemed to know. Karen was the only person I'd told. They hadn't found out by telepathy. Karen had told everyone.

Exercise 4

Part 3

Maybe when I heard the girl say 'That's her. Her mother's got AIDS.' I should have said. 'She hasn't actually, she's just HIV positive but even if she had two heads, it's none of your business.' I didn't though. I felt so betrayed by Karen. I wanted to go round to her house, force her to confess then go mad at her. I went to her house, her mother answered the door. She was really hostile. She told me not to contact Karen or come to the house. She talked to me like I was rubbish. It wasn't fair. When Julia Robinson's mother was ill everyone had been so nice to her. I was being treated like a criminal by Karen's mum. Unfortunately for Karen it was impossible for her to avoid me. She denied telling anyone at first. It was obvious she was lying. After a few minutes she admitted she'd told her mother and her mother had told everyone else's mother. She did keep saying she was really sorry and I kind of believed her. Whether I did or not, I had to learn to live with the fact that my mother's HIV status was common knowledge. That evening I asked mum if I could change schools. She wanted to know why, then after a few days she guessed why. She said she would talk to my teachers but that she also thought it would be good to go to a group. I asked her what she meant and she said there was a group specially for kids whose family members are HIV positive. It took me another month before I went but I decided I still wanted to talk to other people and this time I wanted to choose people who were in the same situation so that they would really understand. When I got there a young woman welcomed me. She seemed very friendly and told me I could just listen to other people talking if I didn't want to join in. I looked around the room, then suddenly I saw someone I knew. She looked really embarrassed. I told her about my mum and she told me about her older brother. She said the group was good because you could just go there to chat or talk about your problems. The group even held parties and had special weekend activities. In a funny way it's brought me and mum closer. I used to think the virus was our biggest problem, now I know that it can be controlled with drugs. Our biggest problem is people's prejudice and we can deal with that too.

16 Getting a Job as an Au Pair

Exercise 2

Mr Palin: Hello.

Tania: Oh, hello. Is that Mr Palin? My name's Tania Brinkhouse. I'm ringing about the au pair job. The agency told me to give you a call.

Mr Palin: Oh, hello Tania, yes they said you'd call this evening. Now obviously it would be good to make an appointment for you to come round and see the kids to see if you like them and they like you.

Tania: Sure. When would suit you?

Mr Palin: Is Thursday OK with you?

Tania: Well, I usually go to evening classes on a Thursday but I suppose I could… .

Mr Palin: No no … don't worry. How about Wednesday?

Tania: That would be better – if that's OK with you.

Mr Palin: No problem.

Tania: What time would be good for you?

Mr Palin: Well obviously my wife and I work during the day. We both get back at about six. The kids eat at about six thirty. Then they play for a little bit … tell you what, would you like to come round at about seven o' clock or is that a bit late for you?

Tania: Seven's fine.

Mr Palin: Ok, that's perfect, I'll tell my wife. Wednesday at seven … before you meet us though, are there any questions you'd like to ask now?

Tania: Yes, I was just going to check the details that the agency gave me.

Mr Palin: OK

Tania: Your son is five and your daughter's six, is that right?

Mr Palin: Yes, although she'll be seven in three weeks' time and is counting the days and hours till her birthday.

Tania: aah …

Mr Palin: Have you looked after children a lot?

Tania: Quite a lot. I'm the oldest of five. And I taught small children drama when I was at school. I did it as part of my work experience because I want to be a primary school teacher.

Mr Palin: That's good.

Tania: Yes, I enjoyed it. Can I check, the hours I'd be expected to work?

Mr Palin: Yes of course. You would need to help the children get dressed, give them breakfast and take them to school. They get up at 8 or before.

Tania: What time do they need to be at school?

Mr Palin: A quarter past nine. The school's a five-minute drive away so you need to leave here at ten past at the latest.

Tania: No problem. Then they need to be collected at what time?

Mr Palin: At about three o' clock. It varies because sometimes they do another activities after school.

Tania: OK. And then I need to look after them until what time?

Mr Palin: Until we get home at six.

Tania: And do you need me to babysit some nights?

Mr Palin: Yes, two nights a week but the other nights you don't need to.

Tania: And I have my own room.

Mr Palin: Yes, I'm afraid it's quite small but it's got its own bathroom.

Tania: That all sounds fine.

Mr Palin: Good. Well we look forward to seeing you on Thursday.

Tania: Wasn't it Wednesday?

Mr Palin: Yes, sorry I meant Wednesday.

Tania: And what's the address?

Mr Palin: Of course, yes, sorry. I thought the agency had given it to you. Do you have a pen?

Tania: Yes.

Mr Palin: It's 98 …

Tania: Ninety-eight.

Mr Palin: Devonshire Road

Tania: Devonshire?

Mr Palin: Yes, Devonshire – D–e–v–o–n–s–h–i–r–e Road.

Tania: Uh huh. I don't know London very well. Is it near a station?

Mr Palin: Yes, it's on the tube. The nearest station is Turnham Green.

Tania: Sorry.

Mr Palin: Turnham Green. It's on the district line. You spell Turnham T–U–R–N–H–A–M and then it's green like the colour.

Tania: T–U–R–N–H–A–M. Green. OK.

Mr Palin: Give us a call if you get lost or if you want us to collect you from the station, we will. Definitely give us a call if it's raining.

Tania: Thanks very much.

Mr Palin: See you Tania. Take care.

17 New Zealand

Exercises 2 and 3

Letter number 1

Adam: Hi Mum, I arrived safely on the South Island in Christchurch. You'll never guess what happened at the airport! The Kiwi customs officer asked if I had walking boots in my bag. I said yes. Then he asked me if they had mud on them. I said yes. He immediately looked at them and asked if he could clean them for me. I was delighted! When he brought them back they looked like new. I thought he was just being nice but the thing is New Zealand relies so much on agriculture that they make sure that it is kept safe by preventing any diseases from being carried into the country. Must go now.
Love Adam

Letter number 2

Adam: Hello Jerome, How are you? New Zealand is so beautiful but the amazing thing is we've seen so many sheep and so few people. We hired a car yesterday and drove to the Fox's Glacier. The ice on it was so blue. We did the typical tourist thing and hired a helicopter to go to the top. It was awesome! I think my friend Nicola is missing London nightlife a bit. Here people go to bed early so they can see natural things during the day. This evening Nicola said, 'I just want to go clubbing!' She'll be pleased when we get to Queenstown. Miss everyone back home. Wish you were here.
Love Adam

Letter number 3.

Adam: Hi Amanda! Queenstown is amazing. There are millions of things to do – most of them quite scary. I've already done white water rafting and paragliding and tomorrow, I'm doing a bungee jump. I'm not sure why. But at least I don't have to get up too early because if I'm bungee jumping at midday, I certainly don't think I'll have breakfast! In fact I already feel sick. I wasn't going to do a bungee jump but Nicola and her boyfriend Bennett did one the other day and said it was fantastic. I might also go white water rafting at night. They call this black water rafting. Hopefully see you again! Adam

Letter number 4.

Adam: Hi Juliet! Am having a whale of a time! No honestly, I really am because I've been whale watching. I'm in Kaikoura. The main attraction here is the sperm whale. Did you know the sperm whale has the largest brain of any animal? I know I know, all these years we thought the largest brain belonged to a member of a boyband! The whales were just H U G E. We just saw its huge dorsal fin. The next day we went swimming with dolphins. It was amazing, they come so close. They play for a bit then suddenly leave. It was fab. Will write again soon. Adam

Letter number 5.

Adam: Dear Sam, How are you? This place stinks!! It really does. Mind you, it's supposed to. It's called Rotorua and it smells of bad eggs. The smell is from the natural mud which gets hot from under the ground and bubbles. You can sit in it. it's good for you. But the sulphur in the mud makes it smell disgusting. I'm a bit afraid I will always smell this bad! Anyway, see you soon. Adam

18 Love isn't easy

Exercise 2

Letter 1

Dear Teen, I've been going out with my girlfriend for six months now and we are getting on well. The problem is that when I say that I'm busy or I'm going to play football or go round to a friend's house without her, she doesn't like it. She accuses me of not liking her. Last week she was unhappy that I wasn't seeing her on Friday night. It was my friend's birthday and he wanted to go go-karting. Just us boys – because we wanted to mess about. My girlfriend was so upset that she made me lie to him and tell him I felt ill so I could see her instead. I shouldn't have done it, I feel bad for lying to my friend. She wants me to promise to do it again next week, instead of going to the cinema with my mates. I'm scared that she will split up with me if I say no. What should I do?

Letter 2

Dear Teen, I'm in love with my best friend's boyfriend. We have known each other for a long time and have talked together a lot. He's fun, good-looking, and really nice. I know he likes me too. He told me so. He says he will split up with my friend if I go out with him. The thing is that I know my best friend will never talk to me ever again if I do this. People tell me that friendship is for ever and boyfriends are temporary but I think about him all the time.

Letter 3

Dear Teen, My girlfriend is extremely beautiful. The problem is that a lot of boys ask her out. I know that she tells them she's going out with me but I find it very annoying. She sort of flirts with a lot of other boys. Should I ask her to stop or is that asking too much? Do I have a right to ask that?

Letter 4

Dear Teen, There is a girl in my class who I like but she is not at all popular. When my friend asked me if I liked her, I said no. He keeps joking that I do. She's very quiet but I like talking to her. I think if I went out with her, my friends would never stop laughing at me. They might also be a bit rude to her. They are all crazy extroverts and she is incredibly shy and people laugh at her because she doesn't wear fashionable clothes. The worst thing is that a week ago, she was really close by and my friend said to me as a joke 'Do you fancy Annette?' I was embarrassed so I said 'No, of course not, do you think I'm mad?' I think she heard me.

19 Stress

Exercise 2

Sally: So Lisa, what stresses you?

Lisa: Not much actually! I think I'm quite relaxed. I'm relatively laid-back.

Sally: So you're not particularly stressed?

Lisa: Well. There are the usual stresses that all teens have.

Sally: Such as?

Lisa: Schoolwork – we seem to get loads of homework and assignments.

Sally: You have a lot?

Lisa: Yes. Particularly this year because it's the year I do my GCSEs. So my mum keeps asking me every two minutes how it's going. I know she wants to help but she stresses me a bit.

Sally: Why's that?

Lisa: Well, I'm the youngest of four children and the other three have all done really well in their exams. They're all at university at the moment.

Sally: That's good. She must be very proud.

Lisa: Yeah, I know but I feel the pressure to be as good as them. Because my brother is brilliant at languages doesn't mean I will be too.

Sally: Oh I see, she expects you to be the same.

Lisa: Yeah. And sometimes I say, 'Mum, I might not do that well in my exams.' And she just says 'Oh don't be silly. You'll get brilliant grades – all the others have.'

Sally: Well, she obviously has faith in you.

Lisa: Yeah, I know but that's the problem. I don't actually want to be a doctor or a lawyer, but my two sisters are studying medicine and my brother is doing international law and Spanish. My mum seems to think I'll do the same.

Sally: I guess she's just ambitious for you.

Lisa: I know but it's awful because I don't want to let her down.

Sally: I know how you feel but I'm sure you'll be fine. Steven, what about you?

Steven: Well, sort of a similar thing to Lisa in some ways.

Sally: Uh huh.

Steven: I'm doing my exams soon but I also run. I train about four times a week.

Sally: That's impressive.

Steven: Yeah, but I don't have much time to do homework and stuff. I also have a part-time job at weekends.

Sally: So you're very busy.

Steven: Yeah, you could say that.

Sally: So do you think the Maharishi school is a good idea?

Steven: Yes, I do. Because I think it's good that a school helps you cope with stress.

Sally: You don't think the school is too, too … what's the word … hippy-ish?

Steven: Firstly, I like hippies. Secondly, I think it's nice that they try and help you. My running coach isn't sympathetic about my exams. And my school teachers aren't sympathetic about the fact that I need to train.

Sally: OK, I know what you mean. You think all your teachers care about is their own subject.

Steven: Yeah. Absolutely. Also, there are a lot of pushy parents out there and it's good if the school can help keep you calm. From what Lisa said, I think she would agree with me.

Lisa: Yeah, I do … totally!

Sally: So do you think your schools should be more like the Maharishi school?

Lisa: Yes. The only thing is I can't imagine my school being like that at all. I think we'd all feel very embarrassed to do yoga together.

Steven: I go to an all boys school so I imagine we'd all be even more embarrassed at first but we'd get used to it. A lot of my friends would try to act tough or joke around but I do think the Maharishi school is a good idea.

Sally: OK, thank you very much, Steven and Lisa.

20 Internet Nerds

Exercise 2

Kate: The other day, I read an article in the newspaper about a boy who started an internet company in his bedroom at home. He's only 16 and he's worth £5 million now. It's amazing.

Duncan: I hope to make more money than that when I start my internet company.

Kate: I didn't know you wanted to start an internet company.

Duncan: Oh, yes, I do. I've been reading about it in the *Financial Times*.

Kate: Have you got an idea then?

Duncan: Yes. Do you want to hear it?

Kate: Yes, please. How exciting!

Duncan: Well, if I tell you, you must promise not to tell anyone else. It's a secret. If someone else hears about my idea, they might copy it.

Kate: I promise I won't tell anyone.

Duncan: OK, I want to set up a business selling English food all over the world!

Kate: Mmmm … great.

Duncan: If an English person lives in another country, they can look up the website on the internet and order the English food that they are missing. They order the food with their credit card and we contact a local supplier to deliver the food to their house. It's a simple idea, like all the most successful dot com companies.

Kate: Mmmm. What kind of food will you have on the menu?

Duncan: You know, the usual thing: roast beef, fish and chips, beans on toast. Traditional English cuisine.

Kate: And what will you call your company?

Duncan: I think we'll call it … English food dot com.

Kate: That's a bit boring. What about er... chips with everything dot com?

Duncan: That's a good idea, but I wanted the name to be a bit more sophisticated.

Kate: All right. How about... 'Home from Home dot com'? Or 'Cucumber Sandwiches dot com'?

Duncan: I like that. It's catchy. You can be the marketing director if you like.

Kate: Can I? Brilliant! But Duncan … how will you get the money to start your internet company?

Duncan: I'll have to borrow it. I'll make an appointment to see a venture capitalist. Maybe my Dad will lend me some money as well.

Kate: I'm sure my dad will lend you some money too. Shall I ask him?

Duncan: Yes, please. We'll need a lot. But afterwards, we'll be rich!

Kate: I think I'll ring and ask Dad now …

Exercise 3

married
relaxed
business
sandwiches

m–a–r–r–i–e–d
r–e–l–a–x–e–d
b–u–s–i–n–e–s–s
s–a–n–d–w–i–c–h–e–s

21 Australia

Exercise 2

Presenter: Number 1

Voice: This is the place where you can see the most amazing coral in the world. There are also incredible fish and you can scuba dive there too.

Presenter: Number 2

Voice: This is a highly popular sport in Australia. You have to be very careful because there can be sharks in the water and the waves can be very strong.

Presenter: Number 3

Voice: This is the name given to the original inhabitants of Australia. When Europeans arrived in Australia, they treated these people very badly and their children were taken away from them.

Presenter: Number 4
Voice: This is the name of the city which is famous for its opera house, its beach and its harbour.
Presenter: Number 5
Voice: This is the name for the part of Australia where not many people live and there is not much there.
Presenter: Number 6
Voice: These were the original people that Britain sent to Australia when they believed it was impossible to live there.
Presenter: Number 7
Voice: This is the name for the enormous rock in the centre of Australia that is a red-brown colour. Its Aboriginal name is Uluru.
Presenter: Number 8
Voice: This is the name for people who move to Australia from another country.

Exercise 3

Sally: Oliver, you've been to Australia haven't you?
Oliver: Yes, I love it. I've been three times because my sister lives there. She lives in Bondi Beach which is really cool. Everyone has really good bodies because they go running or surfing or do a lot of sport.
Presenter: I thought Australians drank lots of beer and had lots of barbecues.
Oliver: They do but a lot of them really like looking good and because the weather is so good, they can train everyday.
Presenter: So you recommend Bondi Beach?
Oliver: Yeah, on sunny days it does get a bit crowded but I love it. It's like a miniature California. The only thing I don't like is that I love surfing but the water can be dangerous.
Presenter: You mean there are sharks?
Oliver: Yes, but there is also a dangerous current so if you can't swim strongly, you can be carried away from the beach.
Presenter: Alexis, you've been to Australia, haven't you?
Alexis: Yes.
Presenter: Did you like it?
Alexis: I absolutely loved it. I went to Kakadu National Park with my parents and we saw loads of crocodiles, birds, enormous lizards … it was just so amazing.
Presenter: How close were you to the crocodiles?
Alexis: About a metre away, but the boat had a motor so if we needed to get away fast we could!
Presenter: Good. And did you see any other part of Australia.
Alexis: Yes, we went to the Great Barrier Reef.
Presenter: And saw loads of fish and coral?
Alexis: Yes, loads. But the best thing was the water. It was so clear and warm and a beautiful blue. And at night we watched cane toad racing.
Presenter: Cane toad racing?
Alexis: Yes, in Queensland they have these enormous toads and they put them in the middle of a circle. The first toad to hop out of the circle wins.
Presenter: Hmmm. sounds a bit of a weird idea but …
Steven: No, I've seen it too!
Presenter: Steven, you've been to Australia too?
Steven: Yes, but when I was about eight years old.

Presenter: Can you remember it?
Steven: Yes, we went to Alice Springs and did a hot air balloon trip.
Presenter: Wow, what was that like?
Steven: It was fantastic, we drove 20 minutes into the desert in the really early morning before it got light then we all got in a hot air balloon and you could see the outback really well.
Presenter: What could you see?
Steven: Just the desert, you could see how vast and empty it was. And we saw the sun come up. It was great. Then slowly as it got lighter and lighter, we saw other animals come out. It was so peaceful.
Presenter: Was there anything you didn't like in Australia?
Steven: Um … mosquitoes.
Presenter: Mosquitoes?
Steven: Yep, I got bitten to death.

22 Holiday Romance

Exercise 2

Asif: Mel, have you ever been in love?
Mel: Er … well, no, I don't think so, not properly in love. I've had a few boyfriends, but I don't think I really loved them. For life, I mean. I had a holiday romance once and I thought I was in love.
Asif: A holiday romance? When?
Mel: It was when I went on holiday to Devon last year. My friend Ally invited me to go away for a week with her and her mum and dad. We went to stay in their holiday cottage. It was really lovely and the weather was hot. Ally and I went to the beach every day and sunbathed. I saw Jack one day on the beach with his friends.
Asif: What was he like?
Mel: He was really handsome. He looked like Johnny Depp. And he was 17! It was love at first sight.
Asif: Did you go and talk to him?
Mel: Oh, no, I was too nervous. But that night there was a barbecue and party on the beach. It was quite dark but the moon was really big and the stars were very bright. Jack was with his friends and he looked really cool. Ally and I started dancing near them and Jack danced with me. He held my hand. It was so romantic!
Asif: This is beginning to make me feel sick.
Mel: Asif! You wanted to know about my holiday romance.
Asif: I know, I'm sorry. What happened next?
Mel: Well, he told me he'd seen me before on the beach. He asked me if I was going the next day and I said yes. We arranged to meet near the beach café at 11. I was so excited. That night I couldn't sleep and Ally got annoyed with me.
Asif: I can imagine.
Mel: The next morning the weather wasn't very good. There were clouds in the sky. While we were having breakfast, Ally's mum said, 'It might rain this afternoon so we've decided to go on a day trip.' I didn't know what to do. I really wanted to go to the beach but I couldn't tell Ally's mum.
Asif: So you couldn't meet Jack?

Mel: No. We went on an excursion by coach and it was really boring. We went to a town where there was a cathedral and some shops. I kept thinking about Jack waiting for me on the beach. I bought some postcards. Do you remember, Asif? I sent you one.

Asif: Oh yes – I remember. It had a seagull on it. So, did you see him again?

Mel: I saw him the next day on the beach. He was going out in a boat with some of his friends, but he didn't see me. I really wanted to talk to him so I could explain what had happened. It was so sad. Ally and I waited on the beach all day but he didn't come back. I was heart-broken. When we went back to the cottage there was something for me – a letter. I opened it and inside there was a shell. He had written a note which said 'Always remember me when you look at this shell' and left his name and address.

Asif: Did you ever write to him?

Mel: Yeah, I wrote to him a couple of times but he never wrote back. I was really sad for a while and then I forgot about him. He's probably got a new girlfriend now.

Asif: Never mind ...

Mel: Anyway, why did you ask me?

Asif: What?

Mel: If I'd been in love? Are you in love, Asif?

Asif: No, 'course not.

Mel: Asif, tell me ... please ...

Exercise 3

1) We went to stay in their holiday cottage.
2) He said he'd seen me before on the beach.
3) We went on a day trip by coach.
4) I bought some postcards.
5) He'd written me a note and left me a shell.
6) Always remember me.
7) I wrote to him, but he never wrote back.

23 What would you do?

Exercises 2 and 3

Mel: Tom, this is my friend, Asif. He's in my class at school. Asif, this is my brother, Tom.

Tom: Hi, Asif.

Asif: Hello, Tom. I thought you had a sister too, Mel.

Tom: Mel and I do have a sister called Kate, but she's not here at the moment....So, Asif, tell me, what's Mel like when she's at school? Does she get into trouble? Is she as annoying as she is at home?

Mel: Oh, Tom! Stop it!

Asif: Well, er, no, Tom. Actually Mel's a really good student. She's very good at maths and music. The music teacher thinks she could write music professionally if she was a bit more confident. What do you do, Tom?

Tom: I'm at college, studying maths, physics and chemistry.

Asif: Do you like music too?

Tom: Yeah, of course – but I don't like Steps or Britney Spears, like Mel.

Asif: What do you like?

Mel: He likes TLC and Mariah Carey. Tom goes skateboarding and he thinks he's really cool. Have you noticed his Tommy Hilfiger clothes? Tom always has to have the most fashionable clothes and the best trainers. He just copies everyone else at his college. He has no personal style.

Tom: What's so special about the music and clothes that you like?

Mel: Nothing – but I don't copy anyone else.

Asif: That's true actually. Mel doesn't copy anyone. She's very individual.

Tom: But she is a bit of a wimp.

Mel: You are always bullying me! OK, let's see how much of a wimp you are, Tom. Listen to this story. The other day, while we were going to the cinema, we saw a boy stealing a handbag from a little old lady. If you saw the same thing Tom, what would you do?

Tom: If I saw a boy stealing from an old lady, I would... I'd call the police on my mobile phone.

Mel: What would you do, Asif?

Asif: I'd probably call the police too.

Mel: Do you know what I did? I ran after the boy and shouted at him to stop! You see, I'm actually quite courageous!

Tom: That was stupid and dangerous. Did you stop him?

Mel: Well, no, I couldn't run fast enough. I'm not a very fast runner.

Asif: So what happened?

Mel: Nothing. We went into the cinema and called the police.

Tom: Exactly – that is exactly why I wouldn't try to run after him myself.

Asif: But it was good that you tried to stop him, Mel. Well done.

Mel: Thank you.

Tom: OK, Mel, I've got a situation for you and Asif. You are at a friend's house for dinner. Your friend's mum asks you if you are hungry and you say yes, and then she brings you a plate of black pudding.

Mel: Black pudding? Yuck.

Asif: What's black pudding? I don't think I've ever eaten it.

Tom: It's a kind of sausage made with blood.

Asif: Yuck!

Tom: You don't want to be rude to your friend's mum, but you know that it will make you sick to eat the food. What would you do? Would you tell her you couldn't eat it?

Mel: Oh, I don't know.

Asif: I'd say 'I'm not eating that rubbish'.

Mel: Would you? I won't invite you to dinner at our house then. My mum would be really upset if you said that.

Asif: Well, maybe I'd say I'm a vegetarian.

Mel: Oh, that's a good idea.

Tom: Yeah and the next day she'd see you eating a hamburger in town!

Asif: Then ... I'd say I felt ill and couldn't eat anything.

Tom: But then you wouldn't have any dinner.

Asif: I'd get something to eat when I got home.

Mel: Yeah, me too.

Tom: Well, I wouldn't. I'd eat it all. I'll eat anything.

Mel: Oh Tom, you're disgusting!

24 Addictions

Exercise 2

Duncan: I saw a report on the TV which said that British women now drink more than women in any other country in Europe.

Kate: Well, I certainly don't.

Mel: I've seen you drinking wine and stuff.

Kate: Yes, but not that often.

Duncan: I'm not talking about you, Kate, but you must admit that there are a lot of women who drink too much.

Kate: Oh yes. After work the girls are always going drinking.

Mel: Isn't that a bit sexist? Why should women be criticised for drinking, but it's OK for men to do it?

Duncan: I'm not saying it's OK for men. I think as a nation, the British don't use alcohol well. I always wonder what people from other countries think when they come to Britain and see everyone drunk on the street on a Friday night. It's so embarrassing, and not a very good advertisement for this country.

Kate: It should get better now that the government has changed the laws about when pubs close. They are open much later now, aren't they?

Mel: Why does that make a difference?

Kate: People always used to drink more before the pub closed at 11. Because the pubs didn't stay open and people weren't allowed to drink when they wanted, they behaved really stupidly and got drunk all the time. Do any of your friends drink, Mel?

Mel: Oh yeah.

Duncan: Really? 15 year-olds?

Mel: Yeah, some people think it's really cool to drink lager or alcopops. If there's a party, people try to go and buy alcohol from the off-licence. Most of them don't get served because they don't look 18. But if they do get served, they buy alcohol for the people who look too young to buy it themselves.

Duncan: Is it mainly boys or girls?

Mel: Boys, mainly, but some girls as well. So, if they legalise other drugs will that stop people from taking them?

Duncan: That's a more difficult question.

Kate: I don't think it is. In my opinion, if they legalised all drugs, then some people who are already addicted would be able to find help more easily.

Mel: How?

Kate: The doctor could prescribe the drug to them so they don't have to buy it from drug dealers. One of the main problems for addicts is finding money for their drugs. They often turn to crime. That's why a lot of drug addicts are homeless.

Duncan: I don't agree with you, Kate. If drugs were legalised, a lot more people would take them.

Kate: They wouldn't. I wouldn't.

Mel: Nor would I.

Duncan: Kate, you've drunk alcohol, haven't you?

Kate: Yes.

Duncan: So if you could buy other drugs, you'd take them too.

Kate: No, I wouldn't! I feel totally differently about other drugs.

Mel: I think Duncan's right. Look at cigarettes! Lots of people smoke!

Kate: Yes, but fewer people smoke now that we have more understanding of what cigarettes do to our health.

Duncan: But a lot of people try them and then give up. Giving up smoking isn't as difficult as giving up heroin.

Kate: But I don't think people would try heroin.

Duncan: Rubbish! Of course they would.....

Exercise 3

drinking
criticised
advertisement
later
wanted
difficult
closed
addicted
opinion
understanding

25 Parents!

Exercise 2

Duncan: Hi Tom, is Kate around?

Tom: No, she isn't. No one's around, no one at all, only me, and I'm sure you won't want to talk to me.

Duncan: Oh no, Tom, I'd be, er, happy to talk to you. Hey, what's the matter? You look really glum.

Tom: Nothing. I'm fine, Duncan. I'll tell Kate you called, OK?

Duncan: Look, Tom, I'm thirsty and tired. I really need a drink, a coffee or something. Can I come in and have a coffee with you?

Tom: Yeah, yeah, come in. I'll make one.

Duncan: Thanks. That's great. Hey, Tom, how's college?

Tom: It's OK.

Duncan: Is your work going well?

Tom: Yeah, it's fine.

Duncan: Good.

Tom: I just wish that mum and dad would leave me alone.

Duncan: Are they giving you a hard time?

Tom: Nothing I do is right.

Duncan: What's happened?

Tom: They're always hassling me. Every night they go on at me about playing my music too loud. My mum is always saying that my hair is too long or too short, and she's always taking me out to buy horrible clothes that I don't want. I only want the clothes that I like and I wish mum would let me make my own decisions. If I wanted her advice I'd have asked for it before. She lets the girls do what they want because she says they're sensible. Well, I can be sensible too. Last night I told mum to leave me alone and get on with her own life.

Duncan: Mmm... I agree it does seem harder for boys today. But you shouldn't have said that to your mum really. She probably doesn't realise that she's upsetting you. She is just trying to do her job as a mum.

Tom: I wish she would do her job as a mum and stop trying to make me do it for her!

Duncan: What do you mean?

Tom: Well, she's always asking me to do chores for her. Hoovering, washing-up, cleaning the kitchen ...

Duncan: Well, I had to help around the house sometimes when I lived at home.

Tom: But I've got more important things to do. And I don't go into the living room. I don't even eat with mum and dad very often.

Duncan: Where do you eat your meals?

Tom: In my room or at college.

Duncan: Well, maybe you should try spending more time with them, and see if you can make them understand you better.

Tom: They'll just interfere even more if I do that. The other day, dad went on for half an hour about how important it is to study. I know how important it is to study! I'm doing it!

Duncan: Maybe your dad just wishes he had studied harder when he was at school.

Tom: Well, that's not my problem.

Kate: Hi guys. How's it going?

Duncan: Hi Kate!

Kate: Tom, have you left this cup here without washing it? Don't you think you should clean it up? Mum is always telling you to keep things tidy.

Tom: See what I mean, Duncan?

Exercise 3

1) Every night they go on at me for playing my music too loud.
2) I wish mum would let me make my own decisions.
3) If I wanted her advice, I'd have asked her for it before.
4) She probably doesn't realise she's upsetting you.
5) You shouldn't have said that to your mum.

26 Teenage Crime

Exercises 2 and 3

Presenter: Welcome to 'The World At Large'. Today we are looking at the problem of teenage crime in the United States. Our guest, Professor Louise Green is British, but she has worked at universities across America. She has been investigating how to prevent crime among young people. Professor Green, is this a desperate situation?

Prof G: It is certainly a big problem. In the States, over two million kids under 18 are responsible for serious violent crime every year. The figure is much bigger if you include non-violent crimes.

Presenter: What kind of crimes do teenagers usually commit?

Prof G: Unfortunately there are many. Shoplifting, mugging, arson, vandalism ... and in very extreme cases, rape and murder.

Presenter: Do you think there is a solution?

Prof G: There isn't one single solution. After all, there is a difference between a kid who is shoplifting and a kid who possesses a gun and is prepared to use it. All crimes are not the same, so the solutions to them won't be the same either. But some people believe that things can be done to stop kids from considering a life of crime in the first place.

Presenter: What can be done?

Prof G: Well, the first thing is obvious. If a teenager is happy at home and at school, then he or she probably won't get into serious crime. It is important to keep in regular communication with our children. The problems start when the kids stop communicating.

Presenter: Are there any other signs?

Prof G: Yes. If, for example, a child is into violent games or is cruel to pets, parents and teachers may worry. Some kids also write about their feelings of violence and isolation, or perhaps they are very interested in guns or knives. If you see signs like this, it's a possibility your child is going wrong.

Presenter: But we can't watch our children 24 hours a day.

Prof G: No, of course not.

Presenter: So how can we prevent them from committing crime when they are away from us, at school or with friends?

Prof G: There is no easy answer. Some people think that experiencing life in jail can help kids have a better idea of the consequences of crime. Of course, they don't go to a real jail, but a military-style boot camp. Boot camps are still quite experimental in the US, but statistics suggest they are more effective than ordinary detention centres.

Presenter: How do boot camps work?

Prof G: They are similar to military training camps. Kids learn about the reality of prison life. They have to work and exercise hard. They live without all their usual comforts: there's no TV or fast food or music. Ex-offenders educate kids about their experiences in jail. Kids hate boot camps – and this is important. Basically, it's a big shock for them.

Presenter: Do you personally believe that boot camps are the solution to the problem?

Prof G: I think they can work on ordinary kids. Kids who sometimes get into trouble at school, but who aren't really bad kids, can learn from the experience.

Presenter: But what happens if ...

Exercise 4

1) We saw a boy stealing a handbag from an old lady.
2) I'd probably call the police.
3) Teenagers who are happy at home or at school probably won't get into crime.
4) Kids who sometimes get into trouble at school can learn from boot camps.

27 Advertising

Exercise 2

Presenter: *Advert number one*

Voice: Brian could NEVER get the girls.

Brian: Hey Lisa, want to go to the cinema on Thursday night?

Lisa: I'm sorry Brian, you're good-looking and kind but ... I'm already going ... with Tony, he's so fascinating.

Brian: OK, never mind.

Voice: Brian could NEVER be chosen for the school team

Brian: Hey Coach, can I be on the team? I hear you need new players.

Coach: Sorry Brian, I've just chosen Tony.

Brian: Tony!

Voice: Brian was never the star of his English class.

Teacher: Well, I read all your assignments and some were real good. Brian, well done. Tony, your assignment was amazing.

Brian: Tony again!

Voice: Brian felt so depressed he had to find out why everyone loves Tony.

Brian: Tony, how come everyone adores you?

Tony: That's easy! It's because I drink Cowboy Cola, America's most popular drink!

Voice: Two days later.

Lisa: Hi Brian … is that Cowboy Cola, you're drinking?

Tony: It sure is.

Lisa: I was just wondering if you were busy next Saturday.

Voice: Cowboy Cola … irresistible.

Presenter: *Advert number 2*

Girl: Wow! Julie, that is a wicked mobile, it's so cool, it must have cost you a fortune.

Julie: No, not at all. I got it free when I connected to Henderson phones.

Girl: Henderson phones, they're expensive aren't they?

Julie: No way! They're amazing value. I can make two hours of free calls during the week.

Girl: Two hours of free calls? That's really good but do you have to make them after six o'clock at night?

Julie: No, not at all! I don't have to wait until six in the evening to call my friends, I can talk to them during the day too.

Girl: Fantastic.

Julie: Yes, it's excellent but that's not the most amazing part.

Girl: Really?

Julie: The best thing is that I can talk for free all weekend.

Girl: You don't have to pay for calls at the weekend?

Julie: No. So I can chat to my friends all weekend and not have to worry.

Girl: What about text messages?

Julie: They only cost six pence each.

Girl: Six pence? That's sooooo cheap, I pay ten pence at the moment.

Julie: Sounds like you need to call Henderson phones today!

Girl: Yes, you're right if I call Henderson phones today, I can talk to my friends every day!!!

Presenter: *Advert number 3.*

Girl: I do love art galleries, don't you, Frank?

Boy: Yes.

Girl: Frank, look, isn't that the most amazing thing ever? It's a Picasso.

Boy: Er yeah, nice, what's in the next room?

Girl: Not so fast, I want to look at it for a while.

Boy: OK, hmm hmm (humming) – enough now?

Girl: OK, it's worth million of pounds you know.

Boy: Millions of pounds?

Girl: Yes, because the style is so original … oh … oh wow! Frank, look, two ming vases.

Boy: Oh right.

Girl: They are a pair. Together those Ming vases are worth … millions. I must look at them more closely.

Boy: A million for the pair? You must be joking. Oh, look at them over there … they are beautiful, the most beautiful ever, what originality, what style, they are tremendous … look at them.

Girl: Yes, I am looking, they were made over a thousand years ago for an emperor.

Boy: No not the vases … those …

Girl: What?

Boy: Those!!! Those, on that guy's feet.

Girl: Oh wow. They're perfect aren't they?

Girl and boy: Borange Trainers … what exquisite joy …

Presenter: Borange trainers, much cheaper than a pair of minging vases and you can wear them anywhere!

28 The Lost Boy

Exercises 2 and 3

Presenter: Dave was severely mistreated by his alcoholic mother who used to starve him and beat him. She did not even call him by his name. She called him 'it'. When he was 8 years old she held his arm over a gas cooker flame. He sleeps in the garage, if he's lucky, eats leftover breakfast cereal from his brothers. Everyday he steals food because he is so hungry but then his mother forces him to vomit when he returns home to prove he didn't steal food. He must then do chores and not speak for the rest of the day.

One evening when both Dave's parents are drunk, his father tells Dave's mother that she treats Dave worse than a dog. His mother shouts at Dave, slaps him around the face. She then yells at him, 'Get out! Get out of my house! I don't like you! I don't want you! I never loved you! Get out of my house!' Dave finally decides to run for it, hoping his mother won't find him. He is so hungry, he walks into a bar and steals a quarter off the pool table but the owner of the bar, a guy called Mark, has seen him.

Voice: I try to turn away, looking for the front door when Mark grabs me. 'What are you doing here? Why'd you steal that quarter?'

I retreat inside my shell and look at the floor. 'Hey man,' says Mark, 'I asked you a question.'

'I didn't steal anything. I … I just thought that … I mean, I just saw the quarter and … I …'

'First off I saw you steal the quarter, and secondly those guys need it to play pool. Besides man what are you going to do with a quarter anyway?'

I could feel an eruption of anger surge through me.

'Food,' I blurted out. 'All I wanted was to buy a piece of pizza! Okay?'

'A piece of pizza?' Mark laughs. 'Man, where are you from … Mars?'

I try to think of an answer, I lock up inside.

'Hey man, calm down. Here, pull up a stool.' Mark says in a soft voice, 'Jerry, give me a Coke'. Mark now looks down at me. I try to pull my arms into my sleeves – to hide my slash marks and bruises. I try to turn away from him. 'Hey kid, are you all right?' Mark asks.

I shake my head from side to side. No! I say to myself. I'm not all right. Nothing's right! I so badly want to tell him but …

'Here, drink up,' Mark says as he slides over the glass of Coke. I grab the red plastic glass with both hands and suck on the paper straw until the soda is gone.

'Hey kid,' Mark asks, 'what's your name? You got a home? Where do you live?'

I'm so ashamed. I know I can't answer. I act as if I did not hear him.

Mark nods his head, 'Don't move,' he says as he grabs my glass and fills it up as he grabs the phone. After he hangs up the phone, Mark sits back down. 'You want to tell me what's wrong?'

'Mother and I don't get along', I mumble, hoping no one can hear me. 'She, ah, she ah … told me to leave.'

'Don't you think she's worried about you?' he asks.

'Right! Are you kidding?' I blurt out. Oops, I say to myself. Keep your mouth shut! I glance at the two men playing pool and the others beside them – laughing, eating, having a good time.

I wish I were a real person.

I turn my back to Mark.

'I gotta go.'

'Where ya going?'

'Uhm I just gotta go sir'

'Did your mother really tell you to leave?'

Without looking back at him, I nod yes.

Mark smiles, 'I bet she's real worried about you. I tell you what, you give me her number and I'll give her a call okay?'

I can feel my blood race. I tell myself. Just get to the door and run. My head frantically swivels from side to side in search of an exit.

'Come on now,' says Mark, 'I'm making you a pizza with the works!'

My head snaps up. 'Really?' I shout. 'But I don't have any …'

'Hey man, don't worry about it, just wait here.' He smiles at me.

My mouth begins to water. I can see myself eating a hot meal. Not from a garbage can or a piece of stale bread, but a real meal. Minutes pass, I sit upright waiting for another glance from Mark.

From the front door a policeman in a dark blue uniform enters. The two men talk for a while and then Mark points to me.

I know I've lost. I feel whatever strength I had now drain. I so badly want to find a hole to curl up into. The officer walks behind me. 'Don't worry,' he says. 'You're gonna be all right.' All I can think is that somewhere out there, she is waiting for me. I'm going back to the house. Back to the mother.

Presenter: Mark gives Dave his pizza. The policeman takes Dave to the police station where Dave's father has come to collect him.

Voice: Minutes later the door from the office creaks. Father steps out from the room, shaking the policeman's hand. The officer approaches me. He bends down. 'David, it was just a small misunderstanding. Your father here tells me that you became upset when your mother wouldn't let you ride your bike. You don't need to run away for something like that. So you go home with your father now, and you and your mother work this thing out. Your father says she's worried sick over you.' He then changes his tone of voice and says 'And don't you put your parents through that again. I hope you've learned your lesson.'

I stand in front of the officer in total disbelief. I can't believe what I'm hearing. Ride my bike? I don't even have one. I've never ridden one before. I realize this is one of mother's cover stories. It figures.

'And David,' the officer states, 'treat your parents with respect and dignity. You don't know how lucky you are.'

★★★ Students with 3-4 years of English

29 The Environment

Exercise 2

Presenter: Are young people today concerned about the environment? Surely, as the future generation, with responsibility for protecting the planet, it's the sort of thing you take very seriously indeed, isn't it?

Becky: Well, I think we should be, and certainly there's been lots of advertisements on the television recently, for saving water and switching lights off and things like that. I think the problem with our teenage age group, is that because of this adult pressure for us to become environmentally friendly, it used to be cool when we were children to kind of like pick up litter for ourselves and save the animals, and things like that. But when you're older you want to seem cool and like these things don't bother you so much. I see loads of litter dropped around our college. There's loads of people with not a lot of regard for the environment, because they can't be bothered, it's not cool enough.

Presenter: Has it almost gone the other way then, it's gone full cycle, so now it's uncool?

Stephen: I think that when certain people treat the Earth like a person or something like that, and say you're killing the Earth, you're destroying it, I think that that's the wrong approach. I think that people should be told that they should recycle, because otherwise this planet is going to be uninhabitable. So I'd advise them to do it for themselves, not for anyone else, not for the squirrels or anything like that. I don't think that enough is being done to prevent things from happening because even if you think it's not going to effect you in your lifetime, you wouldn't want maybe your children to suffer because you've been particularly careless or selfish. I don't think enough is being done.

Becky: I think one of the problems is that if everyone obviously holds this view, then a whole mass of people aren't going to be doing the environmentally friendly things that they should, because they say, oh, it's just the factories, what can I do, the little I do can't make a difference. With this common attitude, nothing is being done, nothing is being gained so therefore we're not progressing any further in saving the world. I mean certainly illnesses in teenagers such as asthma and allergies such as nut allergies, have been increasing, and people have linked this directly to pollution. So if teenagers suffering from asthma or allergies, were told about all these links, perhaps they would stop polluting because they would be thinking of their own gain, or helping their mates, rather than simply doing it because they're being told.

Presenter: Do you think it ought to be like it is in Germany, where it ought to be the law that you recycle, and if you don't you get fined?

Becky: Yes, I think that would be a really good idea, because I'm sure if more recycling bins were available, if it was as convenient for someone in their household to recycle their products as it is just to put them in their own bins, then people would do it, people would be pleased to do it. It's the fact that people have to make that extra effort to find a bottle bank, or to find a paper bank. Busy working people don't have the time, or say they don't have the time to do this. You know, they'd rather not put themselves out. So they don't. If it was law, then people wouldn't want a fine, and also if the government therefore made more options available to people, I'm sure people would, it'd be a really good idea.

30 Growing up in the US

Exercise 2

Jane: Rebecca, where did you grow up? Can you tell me a little bit about it?

Rebecca: I grew up in a small town outside of New York City called Pleasantville. It was very conservative and a lot of people worked in New York City and lived in the small town because they liked to get out of the big city at night.

Jane: And what's your earliest memory of when you were very young?

Rebecca: I think my earliest memory is staying with my grandmother when my mom was working and we used to go shopping and make dinner for my grandfather before he got home from work.

Jane: And Ila, are your early memories happy ones?

Ila: I have the best memories from being young. My strongest memories are probably playing with my brother and sister, going to the beach with my family, which was a great time.

Jane: Nancy, did you find it easy to make friends when you were a child?

Nancy: Yes, I found it pretty easy to make friends when I was young. There were always girls in my school, in my class, and we always used to get along and ate lunch together at lunchtime and played with each other at recess.

Jane: Were you the sort of person who had lots of friends or were you a 'best friend' girl?

Nancy: I think I always tended to be the kind of person that had lots of friends although, when I was young, I did also have one or two very close girlfriends that I would consider my best friends.

Jane: Rebecca, what about you? Were you shy as a child? How would you describe yourself?

Rebecca: I was not very shy as a child. I'm an only child and therefore am very outgoing so I was always playing with lots of people and being friendly to people on the playground.

Jane: Do you think that's typical of only children?

Rebecca: Yes I do, because you don't have brothers and sisters so you look for your friends to take those roles.

Exercise 3

a) Where did you grow up? Can you tell me a little bit about it?
b) What's your earliest memory of when you were very young?
c) Were you the sort of person who had lots of friends or were you a 'best friend' girl?
d) Were you shy as a child? How would you describe yourself?

31 Humour

Exercise 2

Jane: Rebecca, is humour an important thing for you? Are your best relationships with people who share your sense of humour?

Rebecca: Yes, humour is very important to me and my best relationships occur with people who have a good sense of humour. I think it's very important to not only laugh at jokes and things in the world but also to laugh at yourself.

Jane: Would you ever go out with someone who was very attractive to look at but who didn't laugh at any of your friends' jokes?

Rebecca: I don't think I could go out with someone like that because sense of humour and personality are very important to me. It's also very important to me that the person I'm going out with get along with my friends.

Jane: And do you think there's a big difference between American humour and British humour?

Rebecca: I don't know if there's a big difference, but there's definitely a difference. I think British humour is a lot more dry and ironic than American humour which tends to be 'laugh out loud' or 'giggle' kind of humour.

Jane: What kind of American things make you laugh?

Rebecca: I would say more slapstick and maybe not as intelligent humour.

Jane: Nancy, what kind of things make you laugh?

Nancy: I laugh when people are acting silly or goofy or when they make jokes.

Jane: Ila, what about you?

Ila: I think I laugh at really inopportune times, for instance if somebody trips over something or I see something funny on the street and people don't always agree with me that it's funny but I laugh.

Exercise 4 Party Game

Sally: Here is a party game to improve your English. It works like this. One student gets a piece of paper with a mystery word on it. This is a noun, a word like 'umbrella' or 'helicopter'. Next, they must choose a topic to talk about from a pile of cards. They have 20 seconds to talk about the topic on the card, but they must, somewhere, use the mystery noun. If another student guesses the word, they win a point.

Jane: OK, Ila, here's your word. And what topic have you chosen?

Ila: I'm going to talk about my family.

Jane: OK. You've got 20 seconds.

Ila: I've got a really big family. I've got three sisters who are older than me and so I'm the baby. My father also comes from a large family. He has twin brothers and a sister called Susan, who looks like a giraffe because she's got a really long neck. All my grandparents are still alive but they live a long way from us.

Jane: OK, Rebecca, can you guess what Ila's mystery word was?

Rebecca: Giraffe.

Jane: Is she right, Ila?

Ila: Absolutely.

Jane: Right, Rebecca, it's your turn. Pick a mystery word, and your topic is 'My favourite music'. This time, let's see if the listeners can guess the mystery word.

Rebecca: I'm a great fan of Madonna because she's been able to become popular throughout the ages and she is constantly re-inventing herself. On one of my favourite songs there's a strange drumming sound, as if someone is beating on a saucepan.

Jane: Well, I think I know what the mystery word is … but do you?

32 Americans Abroad

Exercise 2

Jane: Nancy, how did travelling abroad change your impressions of other nations, cultures and peoples?

Nancy: I realised that we assume that the American way is the right way, and everyone needs to get with the times. We stuck out like a sore thumb in some places and too often wanted people to accommodate to us, not us accommodate to the people or places. We expected to have things translated into English, easy accommodations. Most people welcomed my poor attempts at trying to communicate, so I tried to assimilate to their culture, but I spent such little time in each place, it was really hard to get a language and customs down before I had to leave. I liked seeing other ways of living. We were mainly in the large cities and didn't get in neighborhoods much so I don't know much about common life.

Jane: How did it change your understanding of the United States?

Nancy: We are too egotistical and self-centered. 'The American way is the only way to live' - that's such a false statement. We don't know how hard it must be for tourists or foreigners coming in without knowing our language. We need to learn more languages at an earlier age.

Jane: Did travelling abroad influence your own life and decisions?

Nancy: I loved it and am willing to teach overseas in Bishkek, Kyrgyzstan, for two years this fall. I'm really excited to get deep into one race, culture, place, language, etc. I want to get to know the place without having to leave within a couple of days. I'll learn the day-in day-out routine of living in a different country. It'll be so good to have a long-term experience.

Jane: Would you recommend that others travel, live or study abroad?

Nancy: Definitely! Get out of your bubble and explore new ideas and ways of living. I think we get too caught up in our own lives and we never get to truly understand a global perspective without getting out and seeing other ways of life. You also learn more about your boundaries, strengths, and weaknesses. It is essential for everyone to experience.

33 Childhood

Exercises 2 and 3

The Irene Street corner was made doubly perilous by Mrs Branthwaites' poppies. Mrs Branthwaite inhabited the house on the corner. She was a known witch whom we often persecuted after dark by throwing gravel on her roof. It was widely believed she poisoned cats. Certainly she was a great ringer-up of the police. In retrospect I can see that she could hardly be blamed for this, but her behaviour seemed at the time like irrational hatred of children. She was a renowned gardener. Her front yard was like the cover of a seed catalogue. Extending her empire, she had flower beds even on her two front strips, one on the Sunbeam Avenue side and the other on the Irene Street side – i.e., on both outside edges of that famous corner. The flower beds held the area's best collection of poppies. She had been known to phone the police if even one of these was illicitly picked.

At that time I am talking about, Mrs Branthwaite's poppies were all in bloom. It was essential to make the turn without hurting a single hair of a poppy's head. Usually, when the poppies were in bloom, nobody dared make the turn. I did – not out of courage, but because in my ponderous cart there was no real danger of going wrong.

I should have left it at that, but got ambitious. One Saturday afternoon when there was a particularly large turn-out, I got sick of watching the ball-race carts howling to glory down the far side. I organised the slower carts like my own into a train. Every cart except mine was deprived of its front axle and loosely bolted to the cart in front. The whole assembly was about a dozen carts long, with a box-cart at the back. I was the only one alone on his cart. Behind me there were two or even three to every cart until you got to the box-cart, which was crammed full of little kids, some of them so small that they were holding toy koalas and sucking dummies.

From its very first run down the far side, my super-cart was a triumph. Even the adults who had been hosing us called their families out to marvel as we went steaming by. On the super-cart's next run there was still more to admire, since even the top-flight ball-race riders had demanded to have their vehicles built into it, thereby heightening its tone, swelling its passenger list, and multiplying its already impressive output of decibels. Once again I should have left well alone. The thing was already famous. It had everything but a dining-car. Why did I ever suggest that we should transfer it to the near side and try the Irene Street turn?

With so much inertia the super-cart started slowly, but it accelerated like a piano falling out of a window. Long before we reached the turn I realised that there had been a serious miscalculation. The miscalculation was all mine, of course. It was too late to do anything except pray. Learning into the turn, I skidded my own cart safely around in the usual way. The next few segments followed me, but with each segment describing an arc of slightly larger radius than the one in front. First gradually, then with stunning finality, the monster lashed its enormous tail.

The air was full of flying ball-bearings, bits of wood, big wood, big kids, little kids, koalas and dummies. Most disastrously of all, it was also full of poppy petals. Not a bloom escaped the scythe. Those of us who could still run scattered to the winds, dragging our wounded with us. The police spent hours visiting all the parents in the district, warning them that the billycart era was definitely over. It was a police car that took Mrs Branthwaite away. There was no point waiting for the ambulance. She could walk all right. It was just that she couldn't talk. She stared straight ahead, her mouth slightly open.

34 American Culture

Exercise 2

Stephen: It's very glamorous, and so a lot of people are drawn to it, it's basically all that's broadcast on the television, in films and things like that. A lot of the big budget films, well basically, all films come from America. You feel interested in a film if it's British, because that's kind of rare. So most things that are made cool by television, films and music, things like that, tend to come out of America.

Becky: To be cool is to be influenced by America. All the cool food, all the cool clothing, all the cool films – it's a generalisation – but are all American. I mean, being the 'land of plenty', with the idea of the 'American Dream', that you can have whatever you want, I think British people, who are stereotypically supposed to be more frugal, tend to turn to America for relaxation. I mean, America for Britain, I think, provides like the entertainment and relaxing side of British life. But certainly, watching the television, I don't really notice if the programme I'm watching is American or British. I no longer even make the distinction. It's more unusual to me in fact if I'm hearing a television programme in a regional British accent, say in a Geordie accent. That actually registers on me much more than if I'm watching some kind of American soap, in American accents.

Presenter: How seriously do you take people who have got an American accent?

Georgina: I think, weirdly, like when Americans come to England, it always seems the really loud Americans. Like on TV when you watch *Friends* or something, they don't have really noticeable American accents – well they are American obviously, but they don't…But when you see American tourists, they are always so obviously American, and they have this amazing, *really American twang*, really emphasising it. And I'm like, you don't all speak like that, cos I watch TV and you don't speak like that, but then, I don't know what it is…

Stephen: I think in England it can be quite a stigma to have an American accent, because there's a certain snobbery in Britain about the dumbing down of Britain by American culture. And I think that if you do have an American accent in Britain, you'd probably get quite fed up with people making assumptions about you, or making jokes at your expense, that sort of thing.

35 Poetry

Exercise 2

Jane: Nancy, are you a poetry lover?

Nancy: Yes, I am.

Jane: Do you ever write poetry yourself?

Nancy: Sometimes I do, yes.

Jane: And what about you, Ila?

Ila: I really enjoy poetry actually; very different types as well. I really like modern stuff mostly.

Jane: Do you write poetry at all yourself?

Ila: A little bit. I try to do some haiku every once in a while.

Jane: Rebecca, what about you? Have you got a favourite poem?

Rebecca: I like the work of T. S. Eliot quite a bit.

Jane: The poetry you are going to hear in a moment takes us back to a more serious topic, in fact one of the most serious topics of all – war. Rebecca, when you look at the daily newspapers do you read reports about wars in various countries or do you ignore them?

Rebecca: No, I read them. I think it's very important to know what's going on around the world and if I ignore it, it doesn't mean it's going away.

Jane: And would you fight to defend your country?

Rebecca: No, I don't think I could fight to defend my country. I don't believe in killing people especially for political reasons.

Jane: Nancy, how about you?

Nancy: I'd like to make a distinction between fighting to defend my country and just supporting US warfare abroad. If I were in America and people were attacking my home and my country, I think it would be very hard not to take up arms and try to defend your life and your family around you. On the other hand, when the US is waging war on other soils I don't necessarily agree with that warfare because I don't always agree with US foreign policy and how we engage war in other countries.

Jane: And Ila, what about you?

Ila: I don't think I could ever have it in me to fight against anyone about anything dealing with a topic that I didn't believe in.

Exercise 4

Presenter: Conventional wars used to involve soldiers who understood the dangers of wars when they joined the army or the navy. This poem was written by Ho Thien during the Vietnam War and shows how even children can get dragged into the atrocities. None of us can even begin to imagine being in the position of this small boy who is forced to look on as his father is killed. It's called *Green Beret*.

He was twelve years old,
and I do not know his name.
The mercenaries took him and his father,
whose name I do not know,
one morning upon the High Plateau.
Green Beret looked down on the frail boy
with the eyes of a hurt animal and thought,
a good fright will make him talk.
He commanded, and the father was taken away
behind the forest's green wall.
'Right, kid, tell us where they are,
tell us where, or your father – dead.'
With eyes now bright and filled with terror
the slight boy said nothing.
'You've got one minute kid,' said Green Beret,
'tell us where, or we kill father,'
and thrust his wrist-watch against a face all eyes,
the second-hand turning, jerking on its way.
'OK boy, ten seconds to tell us where they are.'
In the last instant the silver hand shattered the sky
and the forest of trees.
'Kill the old guy,' roared Green Beret

and shots hammered out
behind the forest's green wall
and sky and trees and soldiers stood
in silence, and the boy cried out.
Green Beret stood
in silence, as the boy crouched down
and shook with tears,
as children do when their father dies.
'Christ,' said one mercenary to Green Beret,
'he didn't know a damn thing
so we killed the old guy for nothing.'
So they all went away,
Green Beret and his mercenaries.

And the boy knew everything.
And he knew everything about them, the caves,
the trails, the hidden places and the names,
and in the moment that he cried out,
in that same instant,
protected by frail tears
far stronger than any wall of steel,
they passed everywhere
like tigers
across the High Plateau.
Ho Thien

36 Body piercing

Exercise 2

Becky: Well, I have five earrings, and I also did at one point have my nose pierced.

Presenter: How do you mean at one point? What happened?

Becky: Well, it's a sorrowful story.

Stephen: Mum and Dad weren't too happy about it, so …

Becky: They weren't over-impressed.

Stephen: So it resealed itself.

Becky: Well, what happened was that I'd been desperate to pierce my nose for ages, because I thought it looked really pretty, and I didn't want anything too big, I wanted a kind of really discrete little stone. And so I pierced my nose, and …

Presenter: You did it yourself?

Becky: No, no. Actually, beforehand, I'd pierced my ears without permission from my mum, which was actually illegal at the time, because I was underage, but no one asked for any ID from me. I never told her I was going to do it, I just turned up at home with three extra earrings added to the two rings that I'd already got. And she was really pleased, she thought, she said that they were really pretty, and she congratulated me on having done such a useful shopping trip for once. So I thought that she wouldn't mind if I went off again without her permission and pierced my nose. However, she did mind, and it got quite serious.

Presenter: So what actually happened, what did you do then, when your mum didn't like it?

Becky: Well, I took it out, but then she said that it was my decision to have it done in the first place, and if I wanted it then I ought to have it, so I put it back in but my nose was too sore for it. So it sealed up in the end, after about six weeks.

Presenter: Stephen and Georgina, what do you think about it, have you got any piercings or tattoos or anything?

Stephen: I haven't got any piercings, no, I'm not really sure if they'd suit me. There's a lot of people, sort of trendy guys who might have their ears pierced or maybe their eyebrow pierced – well one of my teachers has got both of those. But it's sort of frowned upon in our society, it's another sort of snobbery, oh you know, that person's trying to be rebellious, or something like that. Some people might find it a bit pathetic, but I just wouldn't think it would suit me that well.

Presenter: Georgina, have you got earrings?

Georgina: I've got my ears pierced, but I never wear jewellery any more. Like Stephen, I don't think it suits me, it's not really about anything else. I think it looks really good on some people. I mean there is a snobbery about it, and it does have connotations, of rebelliousness, or the older generation might see it as punks or something.

Presenter: What do you think when you see someone who is completely covered in tattoos? What's your initial reaction to that?

Becky: How painful! Yes, I suppose it would make me prejudiced against that person, I can't really help it. But I think people do get prejudices in their mind when they see someone with a lot of tattoos or a lot of obvious piercings.

Presenter: Do you feel any differently if it's a woman who's covered in tattoos, as opposed to a man?

Stephen: I wouldn't like to say it, but I think if a woman is covered in tattoos, I would think differently about that. Because, men, you know, tough men … it's not such a shock. But if a woman is covered in tattoos, I dunno, it just feels different.

Becky: I think there is still a certain attitude towards the sexes, and I think that people would stereotypically expect women to – they'd want them to be more sensitive. They'd be a bit shocked that she did have such a pain threshold. They wouldn't be impressed, they'd be disgusted.

Stephen: In traditional old England, it's quite unladylike to have tattoos like that. I don't really have a problem with it, I think if you think it suits you, if that's how you want to do it, then I wouldn't be prejudiced against you, if that's how you want to look.

Exercise 3

a) What do you think when you see someone who is completely covered in tattoos? What's your initial reaction to that?

b) Do you feel any differently if it's a woman who's covered in tattoos, as opposed to a man?

37 Clubbing

Exercises 2 and 3

Presenter: Many youngsters want to go clubbing, but are below the legal age to drink. So, do Georgina, Rebecca and Stephen go clubbing?

Georgina: Not often. A lot of my sort of age group, a lot of my friends do it every weekend. It's great in one way, if you're in the mood, it's completely letting yourself go, and that sort of thing, so I can see why people do it a lot. But I also enjoy other more like … you don't really get to socialise that much, I feel, you don't get to talk. Sometimes I just feel like having a meal with someone, going out, seeing a film, that sort of that thing. That's also enjoyable.

Stephen: I'm not really old enough to get into clubs, because I'm only 15. That's not really open to me. But I do enjoy going to gigs, which is quite similar really.

Presenter: Becky, you're just about old enough now, aren't you?

Becky: Yeah, just about, and they're quite free with looking at IDs at quite a lot of the clubs around London. I go clubbing occasionally, but like Georgina I agree, it is difficult to talk to people. I mean it's fine if you want to go and be really energetic and do some dancing, but if you really want a social evening, actually, I think it's better to go out with your friends to a pub where you can talk and still have a good time. Quite a lot of the clubs around London, they get completely packed, and they won't let you out, so you're trapped, because you don't get a ticket to show to come back in again.

Presenter: So you mean once you leave, you can't come back in again?

Becky: Yeah.

Presenter: You can't just go out for a breath of fresh air you mean?

Becky: No.

Georgina: Also, the queues – I went to this famous club called Fabric in London. You'll queue for like four hours sometimes, and the bouncers have complete power just to say no, make up a decision, and say 'no, you don't look old enough,' or something like that. So it's a bit much, sometimes, a bit too much effort for one evening, I just think it's not really worth it.

Presenter: Four hours?

Georgina: Yes, we waited four hours once, and it was January, it was freezing. We just went home. By that time, you're in a bad mood, everyone's blaming each other for being late, and everyone's like, let's just go to a pub again. It's not worth it.

Presenter: Well, you've got that to look forward to Stephen, queuing for four hours to get into a club.

Becky: It's just so much effort, and going to a pub or just going to the cinema is just so easy, and quite often a better social option.

38 Hooliganism in Britain

Exercise 2

Stephen: I think there is a lad culture in Britain, but I don't think it's bad really, I think it's just another fashion that the world's going through. I think that it'll probably pass over, they say that what goes around comes around so it'll probably be New Romantics next week or something, I'm not entirely sure.

Georgina: That's another thing that magazines have created, the whole Loaded lad that drinks beer, like birds or whatever. Women are just kind of objects to them. Obviously some guys are like that, but I don't think it's totally representative of the entire young guys in Britain. I don't think it's anything too much to worry about. Except the violent area, the hooliganism of it, which is possibly the worst side of it.

Becky: I know there is an argument that now our society's become secular, we've got a young generation who don't really have anything to believe in, to put faith in – there isn't anything in Britain like the Church, for example, any institution. So they turn to stuff like football, which quite often interests a lot of lads, and put the kind of faith they might have been putting in God before, simply because that was what everyone did last century, I mean this century they put their faith in football matches. They've got all this energy, spurred by alcohol, I think hooliganism arises from that. Lots of energy, and nowhere to put it.

Georgina: It's probably a small minority that go and ruin it for everyone, as people in Britain are always saying. It's unfair, it's not a reflection of everyone. It can be such a uniting thing. I'm not that into football, but when we have World Cups and Euro Cups, it really brings everyone together. It's really fun, and it's unfortunate that some people ruin that.

39 Careers

Exercise 2

Becky: I love to perform, I really love singing and I really enjoy acting. Ideally I would love a career in performance – there's theatre, there's the possibility of musical theatre, some kind of cabaret, or even radio work because I love using my voice, I love telling stories, and I'd love to be able to do that onto tape. It's really precarious and I'd like to have a career where I was earning money constantly. I mean having a father who's self-employed, he has to take work as it comes, so my brother and I've been brought up on having a lot of income at some points, and then periods when money becomes really tight. I don't want to live my own life like that, I would like a steady income, and I don't think, therefore, that an acting career is an option.

Presenter: So what you're saying is, in effect, money's possibly more important than your happiness?

Becky: I wish it wasn't, but I think if I'm going to be practical, I'd have to say it is. I'd like to live a life with all mod cons, I don't want to be scrimping and saving just so that I'm doing the work that I enjoy – or that I really, really want to do. I think if I can settle into a job where I'm happy and contented, and feel part of a team, and feel like my opinions are valued, which provides a steady income, I think I could be satisfied with that. Even if it wasn't the ideal of my childhood.

Presenter: Georgina, you want to go into acting or performing as well, do you feel the same as Becky?

Georgina: Definitely, because so many people have the same kind of dream. My dad's an actor as well, and I've had the same experience, whereby you can't plan anything because you don't know how much money you're going to have, or a holiday might be booked and my dad will have to get a job, and it's a difficult way of living. But if that's what you want to do, I think definitely that's what you should pursue. But the thing is, nowadays there are some really mortifying statistics, where 97% of actors only earn £4,000 a year from their work. It's kind of off-putting, because there is so much competition, and you start to question whether you are really cut out for stardom. Realistically there's a happy medium of being creative, but being creative in a different sense, or producing or that sort of area. I'm going to pursue it as far as I can, I don't want to look back when I'm a certain age and wish I had, but as adults always tell me, get your education first. So if I have something to fall back on, then I'm not destitute if the acting thing doesn't work out.

Presenter: Well good luck in the acting, both of you. Stephen, what do you plan to do?

Stephen: Like Georgina, maybe something in direction or production, or something to do with films maybe. Not be stuck in something with lots of responsibility that won't really leave a mark on the world. I think that's what I'd like to do. Have something everyone will remember me by.

40 The Internet

Exercises 2 and 3

Stephen: The Internet is not what's important. I think if you can find anything, anything at all, that you want to, I think it's a really useful resource. You need to know where to look for things, and you need to know how to get there. It's not easy, but once you've acclimatised to it, it's like using a telephone or something like that. It's something that's very simple, although I've been told by my dad that the phone bill was pretty huge last month, and that I should definitely cut down the amount of time I spend on the Internet.

Presenter: Oops.

Becky: I didn't know that. I must be a real individual because I am so technically inept that I still have to call Stephen out to help me to log on. It's really pathetic, and I'm the only person I know in this IT-illiterate situation my age. But certainly I get by without the Internet, and I don't think I'm really missing out on anything without surfing the web much. But then I'm not surfing the web so I don't know, perhaps my life would be enriched by the diversity of things available to me there. I used it for revision, for my GCSEs, and that was really useful, to be able to get on-line answers. I found that incredibly helpful. But I don't like the fact that there are so few ways to regulate the truth of the information. And that also, you come up with a subject, you might have to trail through hundreds of sites until you find an actually relevant site. Somehow I'd just prefer to go to a library and get a book that I know, it's been published, it's got there's some kind of verification that what it's telling me is true.

Stephen: I think the research is the same, even in the library you still have to look for what you want, you still don't know if the information is relevant or not. I think the Internet is just like a vast library, and if you know how to get the information you want, it can be really useful. But I get your point about how there's so much that you don't really know what to do.

Presenter: And of course there's the chatroom situation, where you don't know who you're talking to. There's the danger of people going on and saying they're people who they're not. Georgina, have you got experience of a chatroom?

Georgina: Yes, I have, and you have to be careful, it's true to say. But I wouldn't get unduly worried about it. Obviously there have been some awful occurrences where people have actually met up with someone they've been speaking to in a chatroom, and they've been violent. But generally speaking, people do lie, I've lied, I've said I'm older than I am, that I look different to how I am. Sometimes that's half the fun, and if you don't take it any further than that it's quite fun. It's escapism, being someone else, and learning about – I'll speak to people from the Far East and stuff – it's learning about different cultures in a way. If you take it a bit further, like anything, then that's when it gets worrying.

Presenter: In fact they might not have been from the Far East at all.

Georgina: Good point. Yeah, exactly. You do have to question everything. But as long as you keep that in your mind with the Internet, then you should be fine you know.